ICONIC CARS

THE GREATEST MODERN CLASSICS

Kevin Van Campenhout

TABLE OF CONTENTS

PREFACE

This book is the culmination of a lifelong aspiration: a tribute to the enigmatic unicorns of the automotive realm, captured through my lens as they traverse the globe, inviting readers on an immersive journey.

Within these pages lie the epitome of automotive excellence, with each of the 25 showcased vehicles standing as an unrivalled masterpiece from its manufacturer. Encompassing three decades of automotive history, this project transcends generational boundaries, appealing to enthusiasts of all ages, with each car igniting a spark of fascination and nostalgia.

My journey into professional photography was serendipitous. Although I had always enjoyed capturing images of automobiles and sharing them on social media, the notion of turning it into a career had never crossed my mind. In fact, I harboured a certain apprehension towards the automotive industry as it stood at the time. Yet, in the era of social networking, there has been a remarkable resurgence in the appreciation of cars. They have reclaimed their status as icons of style, adorning everything from T-shirts to decorative pieces. Such widespread admiration was a far cry from the climate of my upbringing.

Reflecting on my visual approach, I resolved that any images I shared must elicit admiration. They had to transcend mere documentation, captivating even those indifferent to automobiles. For me, the environment served as an indispensable canvas, defining my unique photographic style. Beyond the car itself, I sought to capture the interplay of geometry, symmetry and contrast, leveraging the surroundings to elevate the vehicle's presence. It was my steadfast belief that such meticulous attention to detail would imbue these cars with added value, a sentiment underscored by the record-breaking prices many have commanded on the global stage.

During my academic pursuits, an opportunity for a professional assignment arose, but alas, I was unable to seize it. So, upon graduation, I granted myself a brief hiatus dedicated solely to photography. Initiating my journey with collaborations with esteemed entities like L'Art de l'Automobile, Eleven Cars, Artcurial or RM Sotheby's, I found myself in the privileged position of encountering truly extraordinary automobiles, many of which had previously eluded me. What began as a professional endeavour swiftly evolved into a passionate pursuit akin to curating a prized collection; each car beckoned to be immortalised through my lens, compelling me to capture them all with unwavering enthusiasm.

In my youth, the opportunity to travel remained but a distant aspiration. Yet, the allure of exploration fuelled my imagination, and within the pages of this book lie the very landscapes and locales I once envisioned visiting. I idealised these destinations, painting vivid pictures in my mind's eye, and it is this idealism that infuses the settings of the photographs featured here. Each image serves as a portal to distant lands, allowing readers to instantly recognise the countries in which they were captured and to revel in the sense of perpetual adventure. Within these pages, the journey never ceases, offering an endless odyssey of discovery and delight.

With this project, I have curated the cars of my dreams – the epitome of rarity, the unicorns among unicorns, vehicles whose mere existence has long captivated my imagination. This collection is a testament to my unwavering passion for automobiles, inviting you to embark on a journey of discovery, to share the knowledge I've gleaned, and to cultivate your own boundless imagination.

Kevin Van Campenhout, 2024

GOODYEAR
Agip
27
Marlboro
FIAT
Agip
PIONEER
AVON

Ten years ago, I bumped into Kevin on the streets of Paris. He had this knack for finding hidden corners to snap photos of passing cars, almost like he had a secret map of their routes and timings.

What struck me most was his respectful distance from those sleek machines. It was as though he admired them from afar, which really resonated with me. It sparked a curiosity to know him better and dig into his work.

When I finally got a peek at his photographs, I was blown away. They weren't just your run-of-the-mill car snapshots; they were infused with his passion and had this timeless quality about them.

It didn't take long for me to realize I wanted to collaborate with him. Together, we've worked on some nice shoots, and seeing our efforts culminate in this book fills me with pride.

So, don't just glance at these pictures. Take a moment to really soak them in. They're more than just beautiful shots – they're a glimpse into his soul.

Arthur KAR – Founder of KAR / L'Art de l'Automobile

Arthur KAR and his Porsche 968 L'ART designed by KAR / L'Art de l'Automobile in collaboration with Porsche in 2021.

PORSCHE 959

A BRIDGE BETWEEN TWO WORLDS

LITTLE BELT BRIDGE, DENMARK

While the structure of the Porsche 959 was in steel and the doors and bonnet in aluminium, the rest of the body was moulded in aramid composite to reduce weight as much as possible.

The Porsche 959 is a symbol of automotive evolution, bridging the gap between the old and new supercar eras. Born in the 1980s, it embodied a paradigm shift, blending traditional sports car elements with cutting-edge technology. With its all-wheel drive system, twin-turbo engine and advanced aerodynamics, the 959 redefined performance expectations while paying tribute to Porsche's racing heritage. It symbolises the harmonious convergence of raw power and technical precision, paving the way for a new generation of supercars and leaving an indelible mark on automotive history.

Part of a Danish collection, our 959 finds the perfect backdrop in the Little Belt suspension bridge, the first in a series of major engineering structures linking continental Europe to the Danish islands and the rest of Scandinavia. As the sun gilds the landscape, the puddle beneath the 959 becomes a mirror, reflecting its bold stance and iconic design with mesmerising clarity.

Before ascending to motoring icon status, the 959 stood as a testament to Porsche's engineering prowess – an intricate solution to a challenge presented by Porsche management in the early 1980s. While the venerable 911, introduced in 1964 and undergoing continuous refinement, faced the prospect of discontinuation, it was only spared from this fate due to the lacklustre commercial reception of its intended successor, the 928. Yet, the question lingered: how far could the boundaries of its antiquated foundation be stretched? To what extent could technology elevate a car born two decades prior?

Porsche's strategic decision to develop its new car through competition led to its entry into Group B of rally racing. This move proved advantageous for Porsche's clientele: sporting regulations mandated the production of a minimum of 200 homologation road cars, paving the way for the inception of a groundbreaking new breed of supercar.

In its evolution from the esteemed 911 upon which it was founded, the 959 drew on not only the robust power of its 450 bhp engine but also an array of pioneering technologies to effectively harness it. Let's begin with its power: the conventional air-cooled Porsche flat-six engine was enhanced by a water-cooled twin-cam cylinder head derived from racing. Most notably, this engine was equipped with an innovative turbocharging system featuring twin sequential turbos, each firing in succession to deliver an exceptionally broad torque range and minimal response time.

The formidable power was seamlessly channelled to all four wheels through an advanced electronic system designed to regulate torque distribution between the front and rear axles. This system adjusted automatically through an array of sensors or at the discretion of the driver, who could activate a button to switch between modes, with a maximum of 40% of the torque directed to the front axle. This groundbreaking transmission played a pivotal role in the 959's triumphs, including victories

The view towards the cockpit shows the widening of the bodywork required to adapt the four-wheel drive to what was the bodywork of a 911.

in the gruelling terrain of the Sahara Desert during the 1985 Rallye des Pharaons and the 1986 Paris–Dakar – a remarkable feat for Porsche, challenging conventional expectations.

Electronics played a pivotal role in controlling the active suspension, overseeing parameters such as ride firmness and ride height through sophisticated Electronic Control Units (ECUs). Bridgestone engineered custom run-flat tyres specifically for the 959, capable of speeds of up to 320 km/h. In terms of bodywork, crafted from aramid composite material (with aluminium doors and bonnets), the 959 boasted optimised aerodynamic efficiency and substantial high-speed downforce.

A mere 337 units of the Porsche 959 were meticulously crafted – comprising 254 luxuriously appointed 'Komfort' models and 29 stripped-down, track-focused 'Sport' variants, endowed with enhanced power output at 515 bhp. Additionally, there were 18 vehicles meticulously assembled in 1992 and 1993 using spare parts, augmented with new speed-adaptive damping systems.

As the sun sets, its golden light illuminates the Kiln Red paintwork of our car, casting coppery hues that accentuate the elegant curves of its body. Possibly the sole specimen adorned in this striking hue, this unique 959 boasts a vibrant colour scheme, complemented by sumptuous chestnut leather upholstery, epitomising exclusivity and sophistication.

The vehicles showcased in the forthcoming pages all draw inspiration from the pioneering spirit of the 959. Its influence reshaped the landscape of automotive engineering, heralding a new era where cutting-edge technology converges with ultra-high performance. Porsche created the modern supercar, a breed of cars for which the pursuit of excellence knows no bounds. ■

The lever indicates G (for *Gelände*, 'terrain' in German) for true first gear, whereas first on the lever is actually second – a trick to pass emissions standards.

The race-bred engine used two turbos to produce 450 bhp – and a water-cooled cylinder head never before seen on a 911. Future Porsches will be inspired by it.

PORSCHE 959 KOMFORT

1986–1988
254 Komfort car produced (out of a total of 337 Porsche 959)
Twin-turbo flat-six engine (2,849 cc)
450 hp
317 km/h

1987

FERRARI F40

HARVESTING HORSEPOWER

HERTFORDSHIRE, UNITED KINGDOM

DK

All the F40s left the red factory, but some were immediately repainted by Pininfarina at the request of the sultan of Brunei, like this unique gunmetal grey car.

The Ferrari F40, unveiled in 1987, made a lasting impression on motoring enthusiasts. Designed to commemorate Ferrari's 40th anniversary and redefine the supercar genre, the F40 embodies the spirit of racing and symbolises the spirit of the 1980s better than any other car. Designed under the direction of Enzo Ferrari himself, it was conceived to be the ultimate expression of speed, precision and passion.

Against the backdrop of a British farmhouse, bathed in the soft glow of tradition, stands a remarkable sight: the Ferrari F40. Unlike its fiery red counterparts, this F40 appears in a striking light grey, making its dramatic, brutal lines more elegant than usual and demonstrating its uniqueness amid the classic charm of the countryside. It's a unique vision of the most special F40 the world has ever seen.

Competition lies at the heart of supercar mythology, where debates rage over speed, power and exclusivity. When challenged by the Porsche 959, with its promise of extraordinary performance, Ferrari crafted a response in a car that couldn't be more different from the German sports car. While the Porsche was engineered with racing in mind, integrating cutting-edge technology and luxurious amenities into its road iterations, the F40 was designed exclusively for road use, embracing the pure simplicity akin to a thoroughbred racing machine.

For Ferrari, the creation of its new supercar couldn't have been more straightforward. Having recently shelved its Group B racing car project, the 288 GTO Evoluzione, which evolved from its predecessor, the 288 GTO, Ferrari simply had to reconfigure it for road use, enhanced by a stunning body crafted by Pininfarina. Remarkably, within a mere 13 months, the transformation was complete. With the passing of Enzo Ferrari in 1988, the F40 ascended to instant icon status, representing the final automotive masterpiece conceived during the maestro's lifetime.

The F40 inherited the GTO's tubular chassis but featured 11 carbon-Kevlar panels instead of the aluminium shell found in its predecessor. The engine underwent evolution from its V8 turbocharged configuration, with a slight increase in displacement and numerous enhancements. Generating 478 bhp, it propelled the F40 to become the world's first production car to surpass 320 km/h, marking a significant milestone in automotive history.

The driving experience of the F40 epitomised purity. Devoid of electronics, it lacked modern conveniences such as ABS or power steering, let alone all-wheel drive. Inside the spartan cabin, there was no provision for a car radio, and the composite panels were left exposed in their raw simplicity, devoid even of floor mats to obscure the carbon fibre. However, air conditioning was included as a standard feature, offering at least a semblance of comfort.

It was initially slated for a production run of a mere 300 units, but overwhelming customer demand, fuelled by intense speculation during the peak of the economic boom, resulted in a total production tally of 1,311 units

Ferrari
DK Engineering

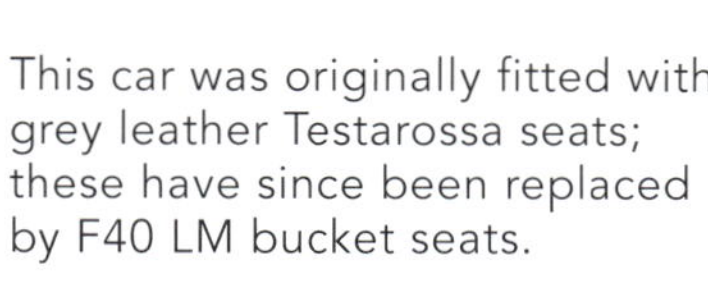
This car was originally fitted with grey leather Testarossa seats; these have since been replaced by F40 LM bucket seats.

The plaque on the bodywork is a reminder that the F40, like most Ferraris in the past, was designed by the Pininfarina studio.

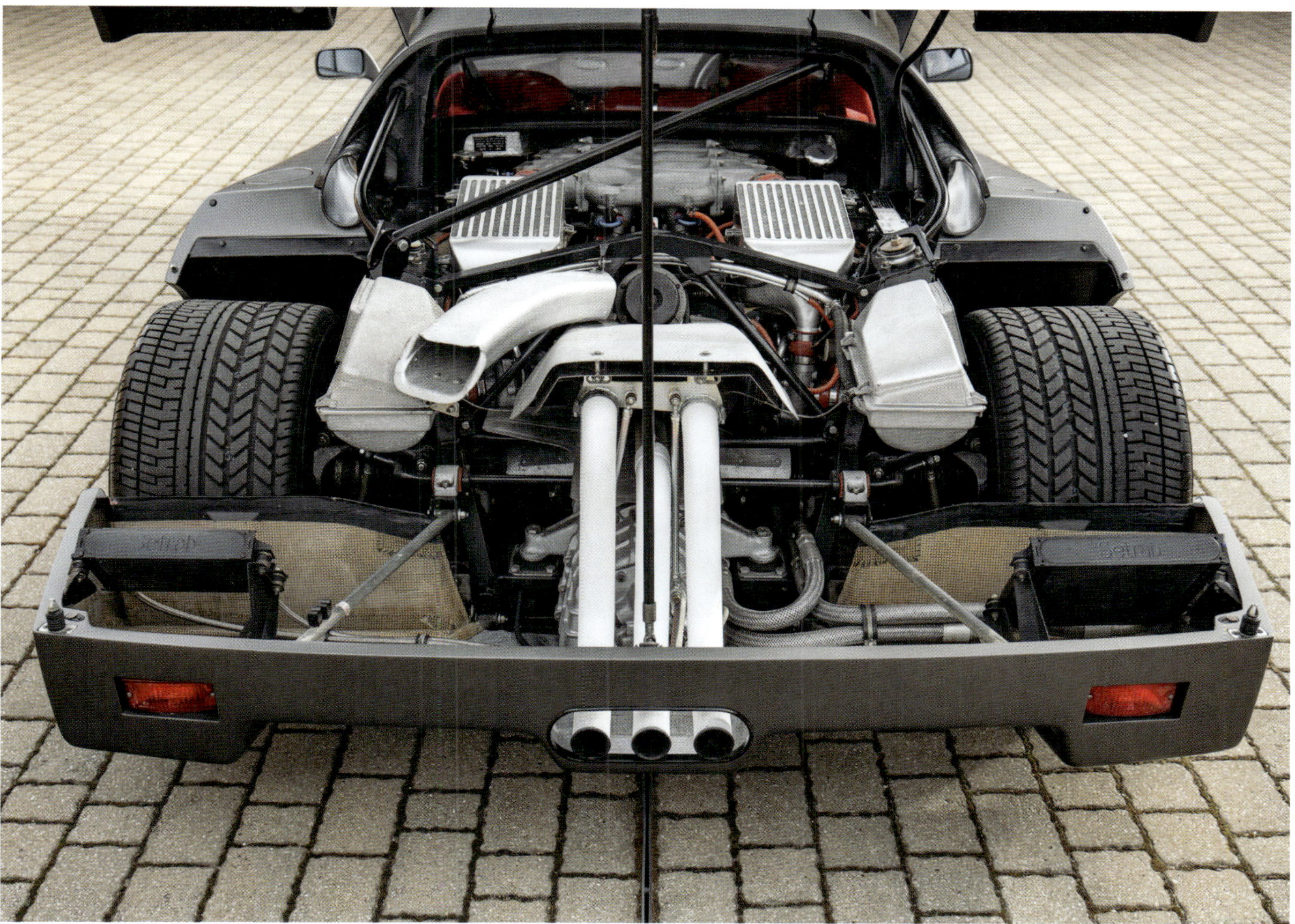

The raised engine bonnet reveals the spectacular piping in the F40's exhaust system: the central tube is used to evacuate pressure from the wastegate.

by 1992. Notably, the F40's exceptional efficiency prompted the modification of numerous examples for competitive racing, culminating in the creation of the high-performance F40 LM version.

Every car that rolled out of the factory sported a left-hand steering wheel and a signature red paint job. However, the sultan of Brunei had different plans. With his substantial wealth, he placed a unique order for seven F40s, each painted in a distinct colour. Remarkably, one of these F40s even featured an automatic gearbox.

Chassis #91283, the car you see here photographed at premises of DK Engineering, the British specialist that looks after it, is part of this extraordinary series of F40s ordered by the sultan of Brunei. Born as a standard car, it was immediately modified by Pininfarina after leaving the factory to the specifications requested by its client: a Gunmetal Grey satin paint finish, and an interior entirely trimmed in grey leather and fitted with more comfortable Ferrari Testarossa seats.

Other features unique to this car included electric windows, a dashboard modified to accommodate a car radio, and a muffler-less exhaust system. When the car returned to the UK from Brunei, it was painted red and its leather interior replaced by a more classic F40 finish, with F40 LM racing buckets. Fortunately, it has since been repainted in its original colour and retains its loud exhaust and electric windows.

For decades, the F40 reigned as the epitome of poster cars, captivating enthusiasts with its timeless allure. Now, as this example returns with its understated hue, it continues to lay down its legacy, evoking admiration with its striking lines and unbridled power – a testament to the essence of supercars that has captivated the collective imagination for generations. ■

FERRARI F40

1987–1992
1311 units produced
V8 twin-turbo engine (2,936 cc)
478 hp
324 km/h

1991

BUGATTI EB110

A NEW DAWN, THE REBIRTH OF A LEGEND

PARIS, FRANCE

The EB110 lines were designed by the architect Giampaolo Benedini (based on a Marcello Gandini project), who also designed the ultra-modern Bugatti factory in Campogaliano.

Unveiled in 1991, the Bugatti EB110 represents a triumphant return for the Bugatti brand. Named in honour of the 110th anniversary of the birth of founder Ettore Bugatti, it marked a renaissance in automotive innovation and craftsmanship. Designed in collaboration with a team of industry luminaries, the EB110 redefined the supercar paradigm with its advanced technology and uncompromising performance. It paved the way for even more extreme cars, pushing the barriers of power and speed to previously unimaginable levels, creating a new genre of hypercars.

In the soft light of dawn, the streets of Paris awake to the majestic presence of the Bugatti EB110, resplendent in its white livery. With the Arc de Triomphe and the Eiffel Tower as a backdrop, this legendary supercar returns to the very city where its story began in 1991, when it was unveiled both in Versailles and the new business district of La Défense.

The prestigious French Bugatti brand died out in 1952, and its rebirth was the dream of Italian businessman Romano Artioli, head of one of the world's largest Ferrari dealerships, who bought the name in 1987 with the aim of creating the most extraordinary sports car ever seen, worthy of wearing the emblematic Bugatti badge.

To make it happen, he had the world's most modern factory built in Campogallianc, not far from Modena, the birthplace of the Italian sports car. And to conceive his new car, he surrounded himself with the greatest experts: talents such as Nicola Materazzi, Marcello Gandini and Giampaolo Benedini were at the heart of its design, as were major companies such as Aérospatiale, Messier-Bugatti and Michelin. Nothing was too good for the EB110, a car the likes of which the world had never seen before.

For the very first time, a production car was equipped with a carbon-fibre structure, a technology hitherto used only in racing and aviation. The new ultra-rigid material was also very light, and the EB110's structure weighed just 125 kg, but working with fibre was still in its infancy, and the Bugatti was a pioneer in the field.

Another marvel of the EB110 was its 3.5-litre V12 engine – the displacement used in Formula 1 at the time – supercharged by four turbos, two per cylinder bank, while the twin-cam cylinder heads housed no fewer than 60 valves in all. It produced an unprecedented 560 bhp (in the standard GT version, 61 bhp for the Super Sport, of which 31 were produced), transmitted

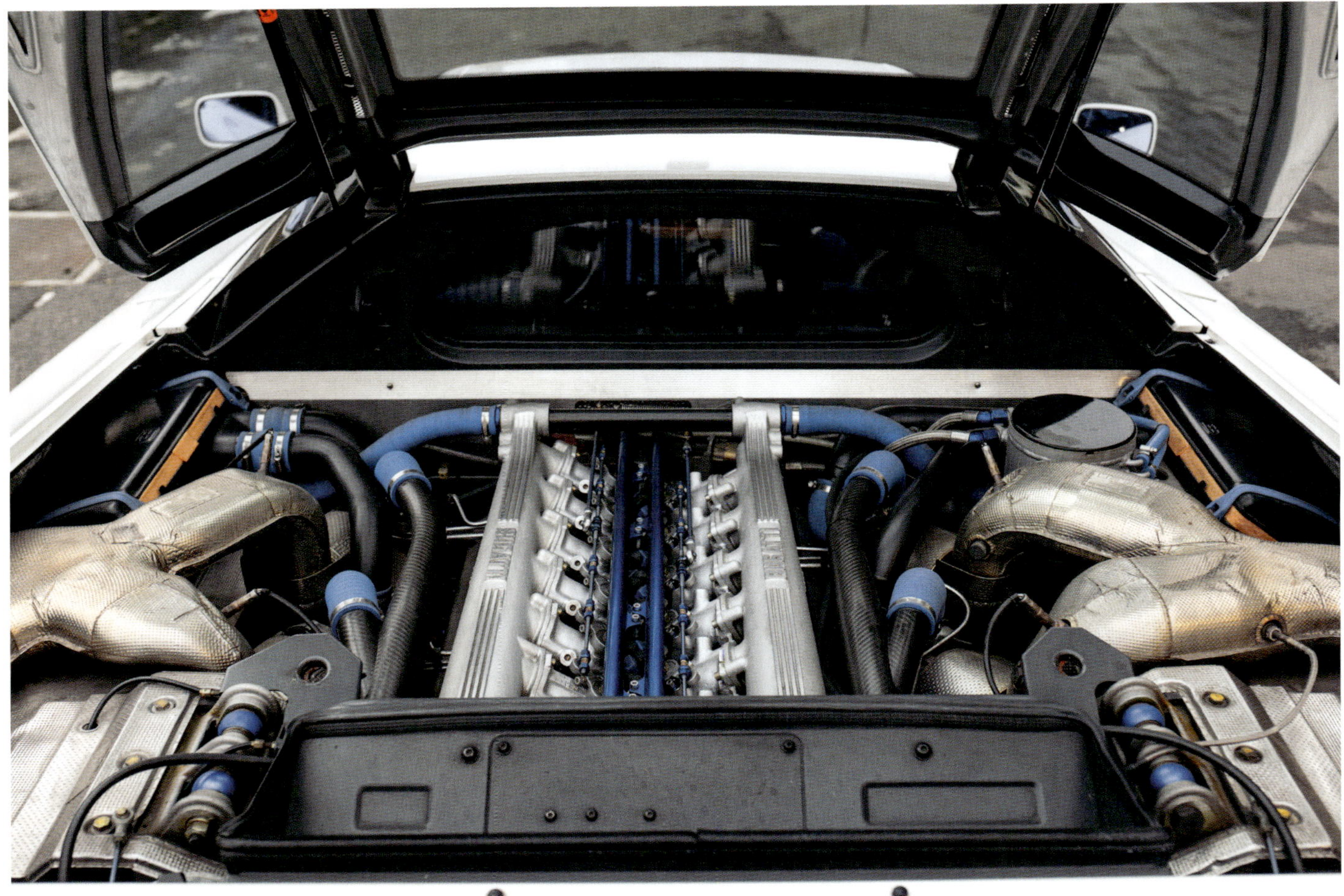

The most powerful engine ever seen in 1992: a 3.5-litre V12 with four turbos developing a formidable 560 hp for its time.

Quite a symbol: a small horseshoe grille, emblematic of Ettore Bugatti's cars, has been placed in the centre of the front end.

A high-tech touch: the 'EB110' lettering on the B-pillars lights up blue when the ignition is switched on.

to the road by a four-wheel drive system developed specifically by Bugatti.

However, there was no question of making the EB110 as demanding to drive as a racing car. Its lucky owners enjoyed unprecedented luxury, with refinements such as power steering, electrically adjustable seats upholstered in Poltrona Frau leather, air conditioning and a top-of-the-range Nakamichi hi-fi system.

Imagine enjoying such comfort while travelling at very high speed. And the Bugatti could go very fast: at 351 km/h, it shattered the record for the fastest production car ever assembled. Among the four world records it broke was the acceleration record, with a 0 to 100 km/h time of just 3.26 seconds. Artioli had realised his dream: his car was quite simply the best in the world.

To launch it, he thought big. On the 110th birthday of Ettore Bugatti, the brand's historic founder, he unveiled the EB110 in Paris, in the ultra-modern district of La Défense, at the foot of the Grande Arche, in the company of actor Alain Delon, before the car paraded down the Champs-Elysées, still accompanied by the French film star, in front of an enthusiastic crowd.

Driving down the avenues of Paris in the early hours of the morning in this EB110 GT, we were able to revisit this historic moment, with a car that has spent most of its life in the French capital (although it is rarely seen: it is the ghost of Paris!). This car, chassis #GT099, is one of the very last GTs assembled. It was bought new in 1995 in Monaco and painted in... Bianco Monaco. It is the only EB110 GT to have received this factory colour, and its interior is equally unique, with its seats in a subtle shade of light grey.

In the quiet moments of dawn, amid the whispers of history and the promise of a new day, the Bugatti EB110 stands as a monument to automotive excellence. Its adventure was short-lived, but it laid the foundations for a more lasting return of the Bugatti brand in a near future. ■

BUGATTI EB110 GT

1991–1995
84 units produced (out of a total of 139 EB110)
V12 quad-turbo engine (3,499 cc)
560 hp
342 km/h

MCLAREN F1

AN OASIS OF PERFORMANCE

MANAMA, BAHRAIN

All the magic of engineer Gordon Murray: no aerodynamic appendage disturbs the F1 car's line – the invisible ground effect takes care of that.

The McLaren F1, unveiled in 1992, represents a defining moment in automotive history. Conceived under the visionary direction of Gordon Murray, it was designed to redefine the limits of supercar performance and technology. With its innovative central driving position, lightweight carbon-fibre construction and naturally aspirated BMW V12 engine, the McLaren F1 captivated the world, setting a new benchmark for speed, handling and sheer driving pleasure.

In a tranquil garden oasis in Bahrain, the McLaren F1 blends perfectly with its Middle Eastern surroundings, its clean lines and aerodynamic profile harmonising with the natural beauty of the landscape. The bright colours of the desert plants provide a picturesque backdrop to highlight the car's timeless design and brilliant engineering. When the sunlight filters through the lush foliage, illuminating the F1's impeccable bodywork, it becomes a true masterpiece of art and performance.

One day, during a Formula 1 Grand Prix, a banner appeared in the audience saying 'Gordon Murray is God'. The rockstar-looking South African engineer had won it all with the Brabhams and then the McLarens he designed, and had become as much a star as the drivers of his single-seaters. So when McLaren boss Ron Dennis asked him to design a road car, his goal was nothing less than to design the ultimate supercar.

With a knowledge of motor racing acquired over several decades, Gordon Murray knew all the tricks of the trade for building a superlative car, but he decided to put his expertise at the service of a strict road car, whose extreme performance should never compromise the quality of its comfort. It would be a pure road car with none of the practical constraints of a racing car.

Murray had been working with composite materials in Formula 1 for a decade by now, so logically adapted carbon fibre for the structure of his car, as well as for the bodywork designed by Peter Stevens. One of the engineer's key ideas was to create an innovative central driving position, to offer the same visibility to the driver as in a single-seater. The driver could be flanked by two passengers, positioned slightly further back.

In order to offer the purest driving sensations, the car had no ABS or power steering, but there was plenty of luxury, with air conditioning and a top-of-the-range Kenwood hi-fi system. Exotic materials abounded, such as the titanium exhaust and the 24-carat gold leaf that reflected the warmth of the engine compartment.

600200

The six-speed gearbox lever is topped by an African blackwood knob, while the starter button is protected by a latch.

The quest for absolute perfection, without compromising: the pedals are made of titanium, leaving their entire mechanism exposed.

This housed a formidable naturally aspirated V12 engine specially created for the car by BMW, developing an extraordinary 627 bhp.

What Gordon Murray hadn't anticipated was the incredible performance his creation was capable of: with a top speed of 386 km/h, the McLaren F1 was by far the fastest production car in the world, and would remain so for more than a decade. So, logically, some customers wanted to race it, and McLaren was forced to go along, despite the engineer's initial wishes. And when the car took part in the 1995 24 Hours of Le Mans, the unimaginable happened: this strict road car, with only a few hasty modifications such as a spoiler and carbon brakes, won a race run in pouring rain. It was a feat that no GT car has replicated to this day, and one that made the McLaren F1 an instant icon.

This F1 was one of the very first to be assembled, chassis #006, and it comes with a unique specification: a Piano Black body, which it is the only one to possess, with a black-and-red leather interior. Another unique feature of this F1 is that the engine valve covers have been painted in McLaren Rocket Red, the same red used on the bodywork of McLaren's Marlboro-sponsored Formula 1 cars.

Extraordinary as it may seem, McLaren still maintains, customises and refurbishes F1 cars a quarter of a century after production ceased, and you can still create a car in your own image at the factory. Provided you can find one: an absolute automotive icon, it is now one of the most expensive cars in the world on the auction block.

The McLaren F1 is one of those cars that will appear only once in a decade, at best. A concentration of the very best in engineering and design, resulting in an absolutely perfect object, magnified by an unexpected and extraordinary event that will make it an instant fixture in the automotive hall of fame. ■

The most spectacular aspect of the McLaren F1 is the central driving position, promising the same sensations as those experienced by Formula 1 drivers. The two passengers are relegated to the sides, towards the back. Don't expect to have a chat.

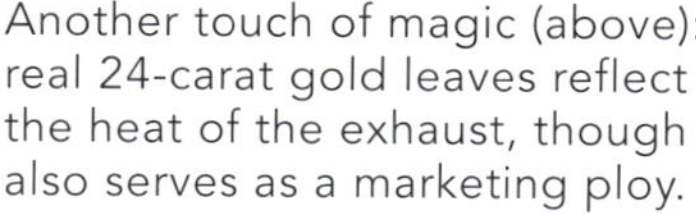

Another touch of magic (above): real 24-carat gold leaves reflect the heat of the exhaust, though also serves as a marketing ploy.

The first car built by the McLaren Formula 1 team evokes the promise in its name: it's an F1 car for the road.

600200
BAHRAIN

MCLAREN F1

1992–1998
64 road cars produced (out of a total of 106 F1)
V12 engine (6,064 cc)
627 hp
387 km/h

FERRARI F50

UNLEASHING THE SPIRIT OF FORMULA 1

LONDON, UNITED KINGDOM

WILTON
PLACE SW1
CITY OF WESTMINSTER

F5 OCG

Emblematic today, the lines of the F50 caused quite a stir when it was launched: never before had Pininfarina's wind tunnel dictated so much to the designers – form follows function.

The Ferrari F50, introduced in 1995, represents the pinnacle of Ferrari's racing heritage and technological prowess. Derived from Formula 1 technology and designed to celebrate Ferrari's 50th anniversary, it embodies the spirit of speed and precision. With only 349 units produced, the F50 remains a rare and coveted masterpiece, revered by enthusiasts and collectors for its unrivalled build quality and exhilarating driving experience.

Photographed amidst the historic streets of Westminster, surrounded by picturesque mews, traditional brick houses and elegant residences, the Ferrari F50 emerges as a symbol of automotive prestige and performance. Against this backdrop of London's timeless charm and sophistication, the F50 is a testament to Ferrari's heritage of innovation, technical excellence and uncompromising performance.

At the heart of the Ferrari F50 was its powertrain, a naturally aspirated 4.7-litre V12 engine derived directly from Ferrari's Formula 1 programme. Indeed, it was based on the engine of the Ferrari 641, the F1 car driven by Alain Prost and Nigel Mansell in 1990, and this choice was not without reason: one of the F50's raisons d'être was to allow this engine to be homologated for use in the 1994 333 SP racing car. This masterpiece of engineering, with a red line at 8,500 rpm, and five valves per cylinder, produced a staggering 520 hp, giving an output of 109 bhp per litre – the best output ever achieved by a naturally aspirated engine at the time.

Innovative construction techniques have played a crucial role in the F50's performance and handling. As in Formula 1, the car's chassis was constructed from carbon fibre, but the analogy with a racing car didn't stop there, as on the F50 the engine was also load-bearing, meaning that it was an integral part of the structure. Directly bolted to the central cell, it supported the rear suspension, benefiting from its lightweight construction and exceptional rigidity, but at the expense of ride comfort: the slightest vibration was transmitted to the back of the driver and passenger, making the driving experience even more visceral.

The F50's suspension system is another area where Formula 1 technology has influenced its design. The car is fitted with a double wishbone titanium suspension system, actuated via pushrods and rockers by horizontally positioned spring-damper combinations, enabling it to turn flat out and achieve breathtaking cornering speeds.

Aerodynamics played a crucial role in the F50's exterior design, with every curve and contour serving a specific purpose. The car features a low nose, streamlined bodywork and distinctive rear wing, as well as a rear diffuser, all designed to optimise airflow and reduce drag. The F50's aerodynamic package generates significant downforce at high speeds, improving stability

The absolute minimalism of a racing car cockpit: who needs a car radio when you've got the music of a Formula 1 V12?

Simple yet effective, the F50's bucket seats offer absolute support and feature high-tech materials.

and grip in corners and allowing the car to cut through the air with minimal resistance. And because its roof could be removed, it was possible to have all this fun with your hair blowing in the wind.

Inside, the F50 is a model of minimalist luxury and driver-focused design. The interior featured premium materials such as leather, Alcantara and carbon fibre, with bucket seats offering excellent comfort and lateral support during dynamic driving. The dashboard was uncluttered and intuitive, with clear instrumentation and controls within easy reach of the driver.

Production of the F50 was limited to just 349 units, making it one of the rarest and most coveted supercars of its era. Although red is the most common of the five colours listed, with the F50, specifications don't dictate price: this car is so extraordinary that its value is sky-high, whatever the colour. First, you have to find one to buy, though, and today prices are ten times higher than they were back then.

To see a Ferrari F50 navigate the historic streets of London would be an extraordinary sight, blending the allure of automotive excellence with the rich tapestry of the city's centuries-old architecture. You'll just need a bit of luck to enjoy this enchanting vision: the English capital is one of the magnets for supercars from all over the world.

True to Ferrari tradition, the F50 was not just a supercar, it was also a thoroughbred racing car adapted to the road. And to this day, it remains the closest thing to a Formula 1 car to have successfully tread the road. ■

For the first time, a Formula 1 engine was fitted in a production car. The V12 engine is load-bearing, and the pushrod suspension with horizontal dampers is pure racing technology.

FERRARI F50

1995–1997
349 units produced
V12 engine (4,699 cc)
520 hp
325 km/h

1996

PORSCHE 911 GT1

A PIT STOP IN PARIS

PARIS, FRANCE

L'ART DE L'AUTOMOBILE

There have been three versions of the Porsche 911 GT1, but this, the second, recognisable by its Porsche 911 type 996 headlights, is the only one to have been marketed as a road version.

The Porsche 911 GT1 Strassenversion, born in the crucible of endurance racing, represents a bold foray into the field of homologation specials. Designed to meet the regulations of the FIA GT Championship, it is the road-going counterpart to the GT1 Porsche's racing car. Introduced in 1996, the GT1 Strassenversion was a limited-production masterpiece, offering enthusiasts a glimpse of the Le Mans car's performance on the road.

Against a backdrop of Parisian splendour, the Porsche 911 GT1 Strassenversion commands attention with its racing-inspired design and raw performance. Parked in front of the historic École Militaire building, it exudes an air of power and sophistication, its sculpted lines and aerodynamic profile reflecting the spirit of motorsport excellence.

This car was born for motor racing: it was Porsche's reaction to the insolent success of the McLaren F1 in GT racing. The second half of the 1990s was a brief golden age for these endurance cars, with the GT1 category offering performances comparable to those of sports prototypes, but with the requirement of using a road car as a base. At least, that was the spirit of the regulations, but while Porsche set to work developing the racing version of its new ultimate racetrack weapon first, the manufacturer kept in mind the constraints of road homologation standards so as to be able to easily derive the mandatory 25 street cars.

There were a few less, but that's not really important. What is important is that this car is the very first mid-engined 911, an architecture that is essential for success in competition, whereas road-going 911s have always had their engines placed in the rear overhang. How did Porsche modify its car? Quite simply by creating a completely new model by assembling what it had available. While the front of the chassis comes from a 993-generation Porsche 911, the rear is from the 962C race car, the legendary endurance sports prototype that won the 24 Hours of Le Mans race in 1986 and 1987.

This approach, which was both rational and economical, was typical of Porsche's way of thinking in competition. Using tried-and-tested components that had already been homologated saved time and money, but also ensured the reliability of the car, which was essential in endurance racing. A key element of the car was its 'Mezger' flat-six engine, taken over from the 962C, and whose foundations date back to the 1970s: it had already won hundreds of victories and was still a benchmark – it would later serve as the model for the engines of the 911 road cars.

However, this meant that the Porsche 911 GT1 was a rather conservative car: underneath its sublime carbon-Kevlar bodywork, which echoed the lines of

911 GT1
L'ART DE L'AUTOMOBILE

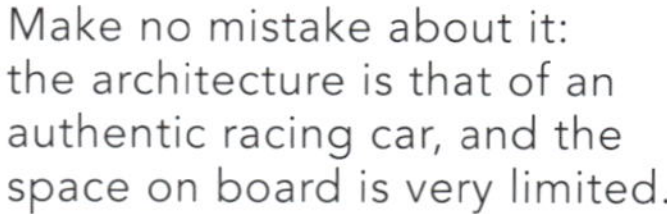

Make no mistake about it: the architecture is that of an authentic racing car, and the space on board is very limited.

The gearbox lever, taken from a 911, has been raised to be as close as possible to the driver's right hand.

Driving such an extreme car on ordinary roads, with such a low muzzle, requires concentration at all times.

The car's body is the same as that of a racing car, with its many cooling holes.

the spectacularly reworked 911s, was a rather heavy, traditional tubular steel structure. And inside, there was the good old dashboard of the old 911s, magnified by the very racing environment.

For a short while, the 911 GT1 was the car to beat: it totally outclassed the first McLaren F1 GTR short-tail racing cars in the few races in which they were pitted against each other. But victory in the 24 Hours of Le Mans was a long time coming. This didn't occur until 1998 and the creation of a brand-new 911 GT1 (the Evo 98), which had nothing to do with this one: it was a genuine racing prototype with a carbon structure, of which the only 'road' model ever assembled was never marketed.

The car you see here is the one owned by the Porsche Museum, which rarely takes it out, usually for communications purposes. Has the 911 GT1 Strassenversion ever been seen in Paris? Not in the last 20 years, until a collaboration between the Porsche Museum and the Parisian firm and cultural brand KAR / L'Art de l'Automobile, which specialises in the rarest and most exotic cars and fashion design. It was a unique opportunity to photograph it in the early hours of the morning in the deserted streets of the French capital. An exceptional moment with one of the rarest Porsches ever assembled, perhaps the most beautiful of all those experienced in these pages.

The fact that it didn't shine in competition doesn't detract from the appeal of the 911 GT1 Strassenversion: to this day, it remains the most extreme road-going Porsche ever marketed, making it an automotive icon for all time. ■

L'ART DE L'AUTOMOBILE

PORSCHE 911 GT1 STRASSENVERSION

1996–1998
20 units produced
F at-six twin-turbo engine (3,163 cc)
544 hp
310 km/h

1997

MERCEDES -BENZ CLK GTR

RACING ROYALTY TRIUMPHS IN THE URBAN JUNGLE

HONG KONG, CHINA

LB RA 297

Never before has a road car been so close to a racing car: but the headlights and radiator grille are enough to immediately identify it as a Mercedes-Benz, not forgetting the star bonnet emblem.

Born of Mercedes-Benz's desire to dominate motor sport, the CLK GTR was designed to conquer the world of GT racing. Introduced in the late 1990s, it quickly became synonymous with endurance racing success, winning numerous victories and cementing its place in motoring history. With its race-derived technology and uncompromising performance, the CLK GTR embodies the pinnacle of Mercedes-Benz engineering and innovation.

On Hong Kong's scenic roads, with uninterrupted views of the city skyline, the Mercedes-Benz CLK GTR glides with grace and authority, its sleek silhouette weaving its way through the cityscape. Against a backdrop of soaring skyscrapers, it exudes an air of sophistication and power, drawing attention at every turn. On the narrow city streets, the CLK GTR navigates with agility and precision, demonstrating its versatility and performance.

The McLaren F1, Porsche 911 GT1 and Mercedes-Benz CLK GTR form the holy trinity of extreme supercars associated with endurance racing in the late 1990s. But if the McLaren was a road car that ventured into competition against its will, and the Porsche was developed by considering the road version at the same time as the racing version, Mercedes-Benz took advantage of the loopholes in the regulations to develop the CLK GTR into a truly unbeatable car.

The German manufacturer decided not to make any compromises when developing its CLK GTR for racing: it was a pure competition prototype that bore no resemblance to a road car – and its street homologation version, which would normally have served as the basis, was in fact developed later. Much later: while the CLK GTR made its racing debut at the start of the 1997 season, the commercial Strassenversion wasn't available until a year later.

Like a true racing thoroughbred, the CLK GTR used a monocoque structure made from carbon fibre and honeycomb aluminium, and the 6.0-litre V12 engine was derived from that used in the manufacturer's best road cars. It took Mercedes-Benz engineers just 128 days to design the new car, with a little help from the competition: they had bought a second-hand McLaren F1 GTR, which they modified by fitting their own engine and a new body, to speed up development and carry out high-speed tests. In competition, anything goes!

And to say they did a good job would be an understatement: with the CLK GTR, Mercedes won the 1997 FIA GT Drivers' and Manufacturers' World Championship titles by winning 6 of the 11 races, in a close duel with McLaren. The manufacturer did even

LB RA 297

In front of the tiny bucket seats are almost the same speedometers as in a good old Mercedes-Benz taxi, but here the figures climb to 340 km/h.

Behind the steering wheel are two paddles for upshifting and downshifting, but there's always a clutch pedal that has to be pressed simultaneously.

A total of 25 road cars were required for competition homologation, but only 20 road-going CLK GTR coupes were produced, plus 6 roadsters.

better in 1998, winning all the races of the season, and again the two titles. Mission accomplished, with panache.

Marketed in 1998, the road-going version used an engine whose cubic capacity had been increased to 6.9 litres for greater flexibility, and the cabin was fitted with comfort equipment such as leather upholstery, air conditioning and hi-fi, and, of course, soundproofing to try to make the howling of its powertrain bearable. This was no mean feat for what was then the most expensive production car ever marketed, with a price tag of just over $1.5 million. Twenty coupés were produced, followed by six even more exclusive roadsters.

The identification plate on our example bears the number 15/25, making it one of the last coupés assembled. Having photographed the McLaren F1 in the Middle East, and the Porsche 911 GT1 in Europe, our world tour takes us to the Far East, to the shores of the China Sea, for the last car in the holy trinity of the 1990s. Whether on the panoramic road overlooking Hong Kong's forest of skyscrapers, or in the winding streets of the old town, this incredible racing machine offers an immersion into the Asian imagination. And how vibrant its silver colour becomes under the threatening sky!

The CLK GTR marked the history of motor sport by its total domination and caused a stir by becoming the most expensive car ever marketed. But this car of superlatives also left behind a lasting legacy: its formidable V12 engine served as the backbone for the development of the formidable Pagani Zonda, a supercar that nobody expected. But that's a story we'll tell you a little later. ■

S
廣告
v.sign.hk
6011 4322
print@sign.hk

MERCEDES-BENZ CLK GTR STRASSENVERSION

1997–1999
20 units produced
V12 engine (6,898 cc)
612 hp
323 km/h

LAMBORGHINI DIABLO GT

WHEN EXTREME DESIGN
MEETS SERENITY

TOKYO, JAPAN

日枝神社

With its racing heritage, the Diablo GT can be recognised by the embossed badge on its bonnet, which hides the radiator air extractor, and its 110-mm-wider front tracks.

The Lamborghini Diablo GT, one of the latest developments in the legendary Diablo line, represents the pinnacle of Italian supercar engineering. Introduced in 1999, it was designed to push the limits of performance, embodying Lamborghini's relentless pursuit of automotive excellence and a first step towards the world of competition. With its aggressive styling, lightweight construction and track-focused enhancements, the Diablo GT remains a symbol of automotive passion and innovation.

Photographed in the heart of Tokyo, between the vibrant energy of its streets and the serene beauty of the Hie Shrine, the Lamborghini Diablo GT ignites the senses with its striking orange hue and inimitable presence. Whether in the bustling metropolis or somewhere more peaceful, the Diablo GT captivates onlookers and enthusiasts alike with its Italian charm and raw performance.

The Diablo GT marked a turning point in the history of Lamborghini: it was the first car designed by the Italian manufacturer after it was taken over by the Volkswagen group, which brought with it unlimited capital and cutting-edge industrial know-how.

To create this superlative, extreme-performance Diablo, the Italian engineers borrowed components from the Diablo GT2, an unfinished racing car project that gave the road-going GT its V12 engine, whose capacity was increased to 6.0 litres. These included its wider front tracks, which called for new front wings that transform the car's appearance, and its spectacular embossed bonnet, whose shape echoes that of the brand's logo, and which hides the huge air extractor of the oil cooler.

The changes don't stop there: at the rear, a diffuser running the full width of the car has been fitted, necessitating modifications to the rear lights. The racing engine, with its separate throttle bodies, is supplied with air by a voluminous carbon airbox, connected to an imposing air intake mounted on the roof of the car. All this totally obstructs rearward vision and a rear-view camera has been mounted under the huge carbon rear spoiler, connected to an Alpine video screen on the centre console – very avant-garde in 1999!

The Diablo GT's technical specifications were impressive: 575 bhp and 630 Nm, giving it a top speed of 345 km/h. At the time, it was the fastest production

品川1000
す・511

Lamborghinis never forget to be comfortable: the bucket seats have deep cushions worthy of a Gran Turismo.

A masterpiece, the 6.0-litre V12 with its independent throttle bodies and carbon airbox is a true racing engine.

Most of the 80 units assembled have been delivered to Japan.

Carbon fibre is omnipresent on the spoiler and diffuser.

car on the market. But although it was extremely brutal, with its race-bred mechanics, rear-wheel drive and diabolical performance, the Diablo GT was also extremely comfortable, with its opulent cabin and leather-trimmed padded bucket seats.

Production of the Diablo GT was limited to 80 examples (plus three retained by the factory), most of which were shipped to Japan. Supercars modified with extraordinary tuning body kits, ultra-wide wheel arches and oversized wings are revered in the Land of the Rising Sun, but the Diablo GT was already so extreme from the start that there was nothing left to modify! No wonder the Japanese loved it, and in 1999, they rushed to get their hands on the car's order forms.

Nestling in the heart of Tokyo's bustling Chiyoda district, Hie Shrine is an oasis of serenity amid the urban chaos. Surrounded by towering skyscrapers, the shrine offers a peaceful retreat where salarymen can escape the hustle and bustle of the metropolis. This echoes the astonishing character of the Diablo, which can be surprisingly docile despite the visual chaos it causes. Like the buzzing Japanese capital, the GT harmoniously blends tradition and modernity, and the vibrant colours of the sanctuary provide a superb backdrop for its striking Arancio Borealis hue.

Opening a new chapter, the Diablo GT takes a far-from-anecdotal place in the Lamborghini family tree. While its spectacular appearance and optimised mechanical components have served as the basis for the latest regular Diablo evolutions, it also paved the way for the new Murciélago, which literally propelled the manufacturer into the modern age of supercars. It's a milestone in the history of the Sant'Agata Bolognese manufacturer, but also one of the most exciting cars to drive ever to leave its factory. ■

LAMBORGHINI DIABLO GT

1999
80 units produced
V12 engine (5,992 cc)
575 hp
345 km/h

FERRARI ENZO

A THOROUGHBRED WRAPPED IN CARBON FIBRE

HACIENDA PASTEJÉ, JOCOTITLÁN, MEXICO

JUSTICIERO
METEORO
BOTITAS

How do you make a Ferrari Enzo even more exclusive? Re-body it with a bare carbon shell. It's no longer a car, it's art.

The Ferrari Enzo, named after the brand's legendary founder, represents the pinnacle of the Maranello-based company's racing heritage and technical prowess. Introduced in 2002, it was designed to commemorate Ferrari's domination of Formula 1 and to push back the boundaries of automotive innovation. Produced in just 399 examples, the Enzo remains a rare and coveted masterpiece, revered for its uncompromising performance and iconic status.

Photographed in a Mexican hacienda, the Ferrari Enzo stands like a masterpiece amid lush stables and gardens. Surrounded by thoroughbred horses, the Enzo evokes sophistication and power, its unique bare carbon-fibre body reflecting the serene tranquillity of its surroundings. In an environment of the fresh-smelling hay and soft rustling leaves, the Enzo becomes more than just a car: it becomes a symbol of harmony between humanity, machine and nature.

One of the most striking features of the Enzo is its advanced aerodynamics, directly inspired by racing. The car's aggressive design is optimised to maximise downforce and stability at high speeds, all without the use of unsightly spoilers. The car makes the most of the ground effect with a wide flat-bottom and a diffuser that press it to the ground, while electronically controlled moving parts adjust the aerodynamic downforce, enhancing the Enzo's dynamic capabilities as required.

At the heart of the car is a 6.0-litre naturally aspirated V12 engine, developed specifically for the car, which delivers a staggering 660 bhp and 657 Nm of torque. Combined with a 6-speed semi-automatic transmission operated by paddles on the steering wheel, this formidable engine propels the Enzo from 0 to 100 km/h in just 3.6 seconds to a top speed of over 350 km/h, making it one of the fastest production cars of its era.

The Enzo's chassis is constructed from carbon fibre and aluminium, resulting in a lightweight yet incredibly rigid structure that enhances agility and responsiveness. This advanced construction, combined with a sophisticated adaptative suspension system featuring push rod dampers, allows the Enzo to corner with precision and confidence, delivering an exhilarating driving experience that few cars can match.

In terms of technology, the Enzo is equipped with cutting-edge systems designed to enhance performance and safety. Carbon-ceramic brakes offer exceptional stopping power and fade resistance, ensuring consistent performance in difficult driving conditions. Electronic stability and traction control systems harness the Enzo's prodigious power, giving drivers confidence-inspiring handling in a variety of driving situations.

The Enzo's cockpit interior reflects its racing pedigree, with an emphasis on driver engagement and functionality. The minimalist dashboard features

TRUENO
RELAMPAGO
RAYO
ENZO DH

Subtle striptease: opening the bonnet reveals mechanical parts in bare carbon tinted red on this unique car.

a prominent tachometer in the centre, flanked by the trip computer display, putting the driver at the heart of the action. Different buttons on the steering wheel control the driving modes, just like in Formula 1. In this all-carbon capsule, distractions are minimal: while there is air conditioning, there is no radio, and even the windows are manual. Yet the sensation of being in an exceptional car is overwhelming.

This example is a little more special than the 398 or so other cars assembled: the Maranello-based coachbuilder, Carrozzeria Zanasi, which works regularly with Ferrari, has stripped the bodywork of its paintwork to expose the carbon fibre, making this a unique car. The interior has also been reworked, with seats and many details in vivid red Alcantara, while the carbon parts in the cabin and engine compartment have been refabricated in red-tinted carbon fibre.

To photograph this distinctive Enzo, we travelled to Hacienda Pastejé, a heaven of peace in northern Mexico City that's home to thoroughbred horses. This architectural gem, surrounded by gardens and water, is the setting for the prestigious Pastejé Automotive Invitational, the most popular supercar reunion in Central America.

The Ferrari Enzo's combination of raw power, aerodynamic excellence and technological innovation continues to inspire enthusiasts and collectors alike, cementing its place in the annals of motoring history as one of Ferrari's most iconic and revered creations. And its legacy continues to this day: every V12-powered road-going Ferrari built since then has used evolutions of the Enzo's Tipo F140 engine, which will probably go down in history as the last V12 to be marketed by the Prancing Horse carmaker. ■

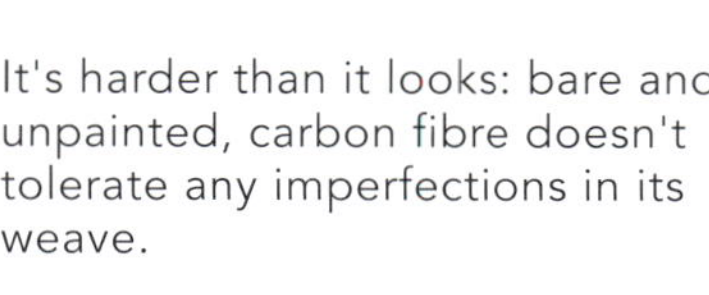

It's harder than it looks: bare and unpainted, carbon fibre doesn't tolerate any imperfections in its weave.

The visual feast continues in the passenger compartment and on the wheel rims, with many of the details highlighted in bright red.

FERRARI ENZO

2002–2004
399 units produced
V12 (5,998 cc)
660 hp
363 km/h

2004

MASERATI MC12

THE LAST TRACK HERO

BEVERLY HILLS, LOS ANGELES, UNITED STATES OF AMERICA

The huge rear wing is a testament to the car's commitment to competition, but ironically, no racing MC12 has such a large appendage: the sporting regulations got in the way.

The MC12, born of Maserati's rich racing heritage, was unveiled in 2004 as a limited-edition supercar designed to compete in GT racing. Inspired by the MC12 GT1 race car, the MC12 road car was produced in a limited series of just 50, making it one of the most exclusive and sought-after Maseratis ever built. With its striking design and uncompromising performance, the MC12 represents the pinnacle of Maserati's engineering excellence and motorsport pedigree.

Photographed on the palm-lined boulevards of Beverly Hills, the Maserati MC12 is a true Italian masterpiece that shines amid the glitz and glamour of one of Los Angeles' most iconic neighbourhoods, symbolising automotive excellence and craftsmanship at its best.

Designed for GT racing, a field that requires a minimum production run of 25 road cars, the MC12 was conceived for competition from the outset. Under Ferrari ownership in the early 2000s, Maserati took inspiration from the extraordinary Enzo hypercar, which served as the basis for this remarkable machine. Although the MC12 can be compared to a racing Enzo, its essence transcends such comparisons. The Enzo's wheelbase has been lengthened, while the Ferrari V12 engine has been upgraded with new cylinder heads and pinion-driven camshafts. Even the famous Ferrari F1 robotised gearbox has been modified to become the Maserati Cambiocorsa.

The MC12 was lengthened and widened to achieve aerodynamic qualities far superior to those of its predecessor, the Enzo. While raw performance slightly favoured the Ferrari – due to its esteemed pedigree – Maserati had an entirely different objective. Twelve variants of the Versione Competizione were meticulously crafted to compete in the FIA GT Championship. This marvel proved to be an UFO (Unbelievably Fast Object), outperforming all other competitors to such an extent that the FIA kept revising the regulations in vain attempts to curb its speed. Despite these efforts, the MC12 went on to win the drivers' and teams' championships 19 times in every season from 2005 to 2010 – a remarkable feat, akin to a major hold-up on the world of motor racing!

Priced at €600,000 each, a total of 50 units of the road-going variant, known as the MC12 Stradale, were meticulously crafted. Distinguished by its open-air configuration, the car features a compact carbon-fibre roof that can be effortlessly removed to indulge in exhilarating, wind-in-your-hair drives. However, prospective owners must make a decisive choice, as there is no designated storage space for the roof within the vehicle. Furthermore, the absence of a central rear-view mirror is notable, owing to the car's lack of a rear window, and the installation of a radio remains an impossibility.

California
12
Maserati

The grooves covering the air intakes are emblematic but regulation: no toddler's head will be able to get stuck here.

Unique materials have been developed for the interior, such as the silver Brightex high-grip synthetic fabric, which is unavailable today.

The MC12 exists in two distinct variants, stemming from shifts in GT racing regulations during its production. Maserati was compelled to truncate the car, resulting in two iterations: the initial 25 MC12 Stradales feature an elongated nose, while the subsequent 25 boast a nose shortened by 15 cm. Despite its grandeur – measuring 5.14 metres in length and 2.10 metres in width – some critics lamented its impracticality for urban parking. Yet, such concerns pale in comparison to the exhilarating prospect of owning a genuine racing car designed for the open road.

The vast majority of cars rolled off the factory floor adorned in white and blue, paying homage to the iconic colours of American racing cars – a tribute to the legendary Camoradi team's triumphs with their 'Birdcage' Maseratis back in 1960. This exemplary machine finds itself in its natural habitat in California. And what evokes the essence of California more than Beverly Hills? And what conjures the spirit of Beverly Hills better than its boulevard lined with towering palm trees? It's a picturesque backdrop that sets the stage for our captivating photo shoot.

Renowned Italian engineer Gian Paolo Dallara, integral to the MC12's development, equated its significance to Maserati with that of the revered 250 GTO to Ferrari – an emblem of utmost importance. Among the most triumphant racing cars of the early 2000s, its absence from Le Mans racing circuits precluded wider public recognition. Nonetheless, for aficionados and collectors alike, it stands as an absolute icon – a testament to its close ties to competitive racing and a poignant reminder of an era when supercars bore a profound connection to the track. ■

Behind the steering wheel, the two paddles operate a robotised transmission specially enhanced for the Maserati, while the powertrain is derived directly from that of the Ferrari Enzo.

MASERATI MC12 STRADALE

2004–2005
50 units produced
V12 (5,998 cc)
630 hp
330 km/h

2004

PORSCHE CARRERA GT

THE LAST ANALOGUE QUEEN

BEAUVAIS, FRANCE

It may be a roadster, but once the removable roof is in place, the Carrera GT's lines become complex: the Guard's Red of this example particularly highlights the engine cover grilles.

The Porsche Carrera GT, launched in 2004, marks a new, more hedonistic approach to Porsche supercars, with deep roots in the brand's heritage. Yet the sexiest car ever produced by the German manufacturer draws its DNA from cutting-edge technologies developed in motorsport. More than a tribute to Porsche's racing successes, it is a true race car dressed up in an evening gown, offering enthusiasts one of the most thrilling and visceral open-road driving experiences ever.

Taking centre stage in a rock quarry, the Porsche Carrera GT captivates with its natural beauty and industrial appearance. Immersed in a mineral atmosphere, its clean lines and bright red colour contrast with the rugged terrain and the black of the stone. Amid the dust and gravel, the presence of the Carrera GT commands attention, evoking a sense of adventure and adrenaline in this raw, untamed landscape.

The Carrera GT is above all the story of an engine: an unprecedented V10, originally developed by Porsche for Formula 1 in the early 1990s, then updated for a sports prototype project intended to win the 24 Hours of Le Mans in 2000, the LMP2000. This project never materialised: after assembling one example, Porsche decided to abandon its participation in the race, preferring to refocus its then limited financial resources on the development of the all-important Cayenne.

But a few years later, just as Porsche's first SUV had filled the company's coffers, it was time for the manufacturer to show off its new-found fortune with something spectacular: a radical concept car reminiscent of the racing cars that made up its rich history, powered by that unused V10 gem. Presented at the 2000 Paris Motor Show, this unique car was so successful that Porsche decided to bring it to market. This was done in 2004, when the first examples – almost identical to the car on show – were delivered to their first customers.

Like a racing car, the Carrera GT uses a carbon-fibre monocoque chassis – still a very exotic solution at the time – but also a load-bearing engine that contributed to the car's structure. The suspension used connecting rods, the brakes were carbon-ceramic and the wheels were magnesium. But this racing technology has been refined for ultimate road use, with ABS braking and traction control offering radical driving performance.

While other hypercars of the time were playing with absolute minimalism for their interiors, the Carrera GT played with the codes of sophisticated elegance, combining bare carbon with large pieces of aluminium

Sleek yet modern, the design of the cabin is enhanced here by the rare carbon pack: black fibre even replaces the balsa wood normally used on the gear lever knob of the Carrera GT.

Carrera means 'race' in Spanish: since Porsche's class victories in the Carrera Panamericana, the name has become part of the manufacturer's mythology.

A mechanical monument: this V10 should have been fitted to a Formula 1 car, then to a Le Mans prototype. In the end, however, it was adapted for this road-going hypercar.

and an abundance of leather. In a subtle tribute to Porsche's history, the gear lever knob was made of laminated birch, like the one on the legendary 917 that won the first 24 Hours of Le Mans race in 1970. Air conditioning, Bose hi-fi and even satellite navigation were included, and the roof could be removed for a taste of open-air speed and stored under the front bonnet.

Guard's Red was one of the few colours available in the Carrera GT's factory colour chart, but also one of the rarest, with fewer than a hundred cars delivered new in this particularly eye-catching shade – the majority being painted in silver-grey or black. To achieve maximum contrast and highlight this red, the car was photographed in a French quarry, not far from Paris, where the incredible destiny of the Carrera GT was once played out. There's something supernatural about seeing the car in this environment: it's like being on another planet. It's not surprising that so many photos of concept cars and supercars were taken at this time in similar environments – and this shot is a tribute to all that.

The Carrera GT has acquired a somewhat sulphurous reputation as a difficult car to drive: despite the elegance of its bodywork, whose purity makes it somewhat innocent, its recalcitrance this testifies to its pedigree as a pure racing car and reminds us that supercars are also mechanical monsters with performances from another world. You have to be humble behind the wheel: it was two-time world rally champion Walter Röhrl who introduced the Carrera GT to the world in 2000, and it was no doubt a sign of the dexterity the car demanded of its drivers. But a new era was about to dawn, in which electronics would soon enable everyone to tame these powerful beasts. ■

PORSCHE CARRERA GT

2004–2006
1270 units produced
V10 engine (5,733 cc)
612 hp
330 km/h

LAMBORGHINI REVENTÓN

A CARBON-FIBRE BATMOBILE

EGESKOV CASTLE, KVÆRNDRUP, DENMARK

This is Lamborghini's first foray into the world of haute-couture cars: with its distinctive bodywork and interior, the Reventón reinvents the Murciélago in an exclusive way.

The Lamborghini Reventón, introduced in 2007, is a testimony to Lamborghini's ongoing quest for automotive excellence. Named after a legendary fighting bull, the Reventón epitomises exclusivity and performance, with only 20 examples built worldwide. Its unveiling marked a turning point in the brand's history, demonstrating Lamborghini's ability to fuse cutting-edge technology with breathtaking design.

Shot against the enchanting backdrop of Denmark's Egeskov Castle, the Lamborghini Reventón features sleek, angular lines reminiscent of a stealth bat in flight; it exudes an aura of mystique and power, like a modern-day Batmobile. As if conjured from the imagination of Bruce Wayne himself, the Reventón has a dramatic presence among the castle's ancient towers and lush gardens, evoking a sense of cinematic grandeur.

The Reventón marked a new chapter for Lamborghini, paving the way for a world of extraordinary automobiles. Described as a 'few-off' by the manufacturer, it embodies exclusivity, built in extremely limited numbers for a select group of discerning customers in search of a unique and personal motoring experience. The Reventón's radical concept-car aesthetic transcends mere transportation to become a true masterpiece of automotive craftsmanship for the lucky few who appreciate its rare beauty and unrivalled looks.

In essence, it wasn't an entirely new vehicle, but rather a subtle re-imagining of the Lamborghini Murciélago LP640, a supercar already recognised as the cornerstone of the manufacturer's range. However, the Reventón was more than just a production vehicle; it was an exclusive haute-couture creation, dressing the Murciélago in bespoke elegance to elevate its presence to new heights.

The bodywork underwent a complete metamorphosis, abandoning traditional aluminium in favour of carbon fibre, inspired by the clean lines of aviation. Resembling a stealth fighter jet with its tapered, angular contours, the Reventón exudes an aura of menace, accentuated by its exclusive green/medium opaque grey satin finish. Its avant-garde front bumper proudly displays the pioneering inclusion of LED daytime running lights, a first for Lamborghini, while the flanks feature asymmetrical air intakes meticulously designed to meet the distinct cooling needs of each side. Guided by the principle of form follows function, as in the aerospace industry, the meticulously crafted wheel designs serve to optimise the cooling of the carbon-ceramic brakes, complemented by a rear spoiler that deploys transparently in three distinct positions.

The cockpit's pièce de résistance lies in its innovative instrumentation, composed exclusively of TFT screens reminiscent of the cockpit displays in a fighter jet. Set within a meticulously crafted structure of machined aluminium and carbon fibre, it offers a driving experience that is both unique and undeniably exclusive. The fully customisable instrument panel features a captivating new element at its centre: a G-force meter, which provides real-time information on the Reventón's longitudinal and lateral acceleration

The Reventón was inspired by fighter jets, and the bodywork and interior colours evoke the world of military high-tech.

Like an aircraft cockpit: the instrumentation (above) was redesigned with TFT screens, including a G-force meter that indicates lateral accelerations.

Is the Reventón as stealthy as a fighter jet? Its faceted bodywork, with its numerous angles and pointed front, seems capable of reflecting radar signals.

Pure functionalism: the side air intakes on the carbon bodywork are asymmetrical, each designed exactly to match the exact airflow requirements.

during acceleration, braking and cornering manoeuvres. This unprecedented representation offers a fresh perspective on the exhilarating sensations evoked by hypercars of this Lamborghini's calibre, elevating the driving experience to unprecedented levels.

In those days, Bruce Wayne, known as Batman, got around Gotham in a Lamborghini Murciélago (the car actually takes its name from the Spanish word for 'bat'). Yet we can't help wondering if, had he owned a Reventón, the need for his iconic Batmobile might have diminished. This photo shoot is a nostalgic tribute to that cinematic link: completed in 1554, Egeskov Castle is one of the best-preserved moated Renaissance castles in Northern Europe today and it exudes a grandeur similar to that of the historic Wayne mansion. But it is just as discreet, its doors having been opened very rarely for motor photography. Such exclusivity reflects the world of excellence that Reventón owners are accustomed to experiencing.

The exclusive ranks of the Reventón Coupés, numbering around 20, have been complemented by a select series of 15 Reventón Roadsters, boasting even more formidable power: 670 bhp, a significant increase from the 650 bhp of the coupé variant. These iconic vehicles marked the inception of the extraordinary Lamborghini Few-off line, a distinguished lineage that includes illustrious models such as the Sesto Elemento, Veneno, Centenario, Sián and Countach LPI 800-4 – each contributing to the creation of a legendary series. ■

LAMBORGHINI REVENTÓN

2007–2009
20 units produced
V12 engine (6,496 cc)
650 hp
340 km/h

MERCEDES-BENZ SLR MCLAREN STIRLING MOSS

THE LONG JOURNEY
OF AUTOMOBILE ROYALTY

FREDERICIA, DENMARK

DETECTOR

DETECTOR

The pinnacle of the Mercedes-Benz SLR McLaren series, the Stirling Moss, of which 75 were built, launched the hypercar barchette craze – still strong today.

Step into the annals of automotive history, and you'll find the Mercedes-Benz SLR Stirling Moss – an ode to the incomparable racing legacy of Sir Stirling Moss, a luminary whose spirit permeates every inch of this limited-edition marvel. This singular machine stands as a testament to Mercedes-Benz's commitment to pushing the boundaries of engineering and design, bridging the gap between the golden age of motorsport and the contemporary pursuit of excellence.

In the maritime calm of Fredericia harbour, juxtaposed with the hectic activity of maritime trade, the Mercedes-Benz SLR Stirling Moss emerges as a symbol of automotive singularity. When the lens captures its slightest curves and contours, it freezes a moment in time where speed, elegance and innovation come together. The ambient light of the setting sun paints the scene in golden hues, casting a spell that transforms it into a timeless work of art.

The Mercedes-Benz SLR McLaren emerged as a striking embodiment of high-level engineering – a front-engined coupé evoking the timeless looks of the iconic 300 SLR of the 1950s, reimagined with a Formula 1–inspired nose. It was an intriguing collaboration, where Mercedes-Benz design was crossed with McLaren's engineering finesse, under the guidance of visionary Gordon Murray, revered as the forerunner of the F1 hypercar. Such a symbiosis was not unprecedented, given the long-standing partnership between the German manufacturer and the British team, a formidable presence on the Formula 1 grid. This historic alliance, which predated Mercedes-Benz's entry into the assembly of its own single-seaters, laid the foundations for the unrivalled success that followed.

This distinguished supercar, envisioned as the 'Tomorrow Silver Arrow', has transcended conventional norms by harmonising the cutting-edge performance of its robust supercharged V8 engine with the refined handling of a Grand Tourer. With a focus on comfort rather than time, it invites enthusiasts to embark on exhilarating long-distance journeys. In its opulent enclosure, luxury lives up to expectations, but Gordon Murray's inimitable touch imbues the SLR with racing-inspired ingenuity. Featuring cutting-edge aerodynamics, including an active airbrake and a perfectly flat floor culminating in a well-thought-out diffuser, it skilfully generates downforce. This innovative solution forces the exhaust pipes to emerge from the sides of the car, which is a spectacle in itself.

The Stirling Moss Edition embodies the pinnacle of the SLR line: unveiled six years after the coupé's debut, this roadster was given a complete makeover, dispensing with the windscreen, windows and roof – a poignant tribute to the 300 SLR open-top race car, synonymous with Moss's triumphant conquest of the gruelling Brescia–Rome Mille Miglia in 1955. Configurable as a single-seater with the addition of a tonneau cover, its exclusivity knew no bounds, with only 75 units reserved exclusively for customers who had already acquired the 'standard' SLR coupé.

Yet the car pictured here embodies an even greater exclusivity, with aspects of its history shrouded

MAERSK

A royal seal for one of the three Stirling Moss cars assembled for Middle East royal families.

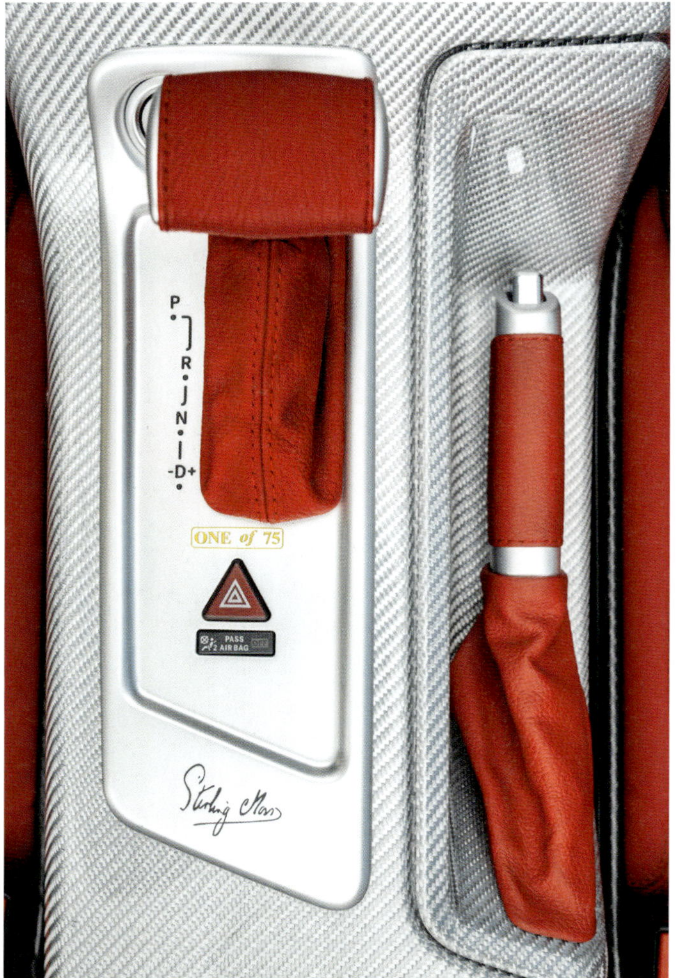

Not only 'one of 75', but the very first one: this is the Stirling Moss chassis #001

in mystery. As chassis #001, it sports grey carbon interior elements, a departure from Stirling Moss's usual black, complemented by bespoke red upholstery – a configuration believed to be unique among the three Stirling Moss SLRs designed specifically for the Middle East. Even more intriguingly, it is adorned with gold plates bearing a royal crown emblem identical to that of the SLR 722 Crown Edition, a bespoke series of ten coupés commissioned by the king of Bahrain as gifts for the royal families of the Arab world. The revelations strongly suggest that our car was originally delivered to the esteemed Royal Family of Kuwait, making it an exceptionally royal and coveted automotive jewel.

With a mere 24 km on the odometer, this SLR Stirling Moss remains pristine, untouched by the road. Capturing its essence in photographs posed a unique challenge, as positioning the car in optimal locations among the cargo ships of the Fredericia necessitated careful manoeuvring. Adhering to strict mileage restrictions, our movements were limited to ensure the odometer remained under 25 km – a task that necessitated the assistance of a flatbed truck. Yet, for this epitome of automotive royalty, no effort was spared in capturing its timeless allure.

An open barchetta devoid of windows or roof may initially strike as audacious, yet it's the sheer indulgence of this concept that elevates it to automotive excellence. It embodies the supercar's superlative allure, appealing to connoisseurs seeking the extraordinary – an exclusive niche beyond the ordinary. It comes as no astonishment that such a design has become a hallmark among supercar manufacturers, a testament to the monumental legacy of the SLR Stirling Moss. ■

Noblesse oblige: this unique SLR Stirling Moss is distinguished by its special grey carbon interior trim and all-red leather seats. Note the 24 km on the odometer only.

MERCEDES-BENZ SLR MCLAREN STIRLING MOSS

2009
75 units produced
V8 supercharged engine (5,439 cc)
650 hp
350 km/h

PAGANI ZONDA CINQUE

THE BIRTH OF A NEW ICON

CANTON OF VAUD, SWITZERLAND

The lines of the Zonda were inspired by the Group C prototypes of the 24 Hours of Le Mans, and in this extreme configuration, the spirit of competition is even more palpable.

Born from the visionary mind of Horacio Pagani, the Zonda series debuted in 1999, captivating enthusiasts worldwide with its blend of artistry and performance. Each iteration of the Zonda pushed boundaries, but the Cinque represents the zenith of Pagani's craftsmanship, with only five (*cinque* in Italian) fortunate owners granted the privilege of experiencing its raw power and unparalleled luxury.

Captured amid the serene winter landscapes of Switzerland, the Pagani Zonda Cinque emerges as a vibrant beacon against the pristine white canvas of snow. The vivid orange hue of the car punctuates the tranquil surroundings, commanding attention and admiration in equal measure. Against this backdrop of nature's tranquillity, the Zonda Cinque stands as a testament to human ingenuity and automotive artistry.

The genesis of the Pagani Zonda can be traced back to the early 1990s when Horacio Pagani, an Argentine-Italian engineer and ex-Lamborghini employee, set out to realise his lifelong dream of creating the ultimate supercar. Drawing inspiration from his experiences in the world of motorsport and his passion for automotive design, Pagani envisioned a car that would push the boundaries of performance, technology and luxury.

Introduced to the world in 1999, the first Zonda left an indelible mark on automotive history, captivating enthusiasts with its unrivalled craftsmanship, an area in which it effortlessly outperformed even the most esteemed manufacturers. At the heart of Pagani's triumph is its early collaboration with Mercedes-AMG, a partnership that saw the Zonda equipped with the formidable 'M12' V12 engine from the venerable Mercedes-Benz CLK GTR. With an initial displacement of 6.0 litres, this engine was later increased to 7.3 litres, symbolising the pinnacle of technical prowess and innovation.

Crafted entirely from carbon fibre, the bodywork of the Zonda epitomised automotive artistry, seamlessly blending functional design cues inherited from Group C sports prototypes with an aesthetic sensibility reminiscent of the human form. The narrow cockpit bubble, suspended rear-view mirrors, double spoiler and deep diffuser all converged in a symphony of sensual curves, each deliberately evoking the grace and elegance of the female body. The meticulous attention to detail extended to every facet of the Zonda's design, from the supports for the small lenticular headlamps rendered in bare carbon fibre to the distinctive arrangement of the four tailpipes, elegantly positioned in a square configuration at the centre.

The cabin has been exquisitely treated to an unrivalled level of refinement, setting new standards in the automotive world. Meticulously crafted, every component is in carbon or machined aluminium, complemented by a range of premium leathers. Evoking the precision of racing engineering, the car's technology featured a load-bearing engine and pushrod suspension, harmoniously combining opulent luxury

Zonda
cinque

PAGANI
Zonda
cinque

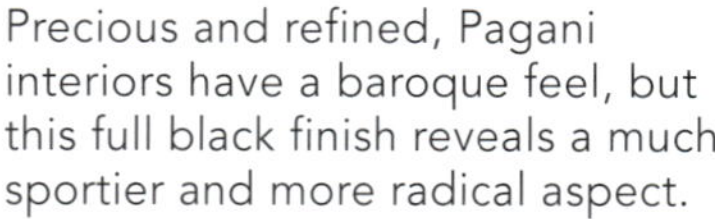

Precious and refined, Pagani interiors have a baroque feel, but this full black finish reveals a much sportier and more radical aspect.

A plaque reminds us of the extreme rarity of the Cinque: as its name suggests, there are only five examples, and this is the third.

The double black stripe of bare carbon and the roof air intake are strikingly distinctive features of the Cinque edition.

The extremely delicate rear-view mirrors are one of the many subtle distinguishing features of Pagani cars.

with high-performance dynamics, embodying a fusion of the most refined elements of both fields. Each element reflects a harmonious fusion of form and function, elevating the Zonda from a mere machine to an automotive work of art unrivalled in its looks and sophistication.

This car's remarkable technical prowess sustained its presence in the market for two decades, undergoing numerous evolutions and spawning special editions, each possessing a unique allure that captivated hypercar enthusiasts. Among these iterations stands the Cinque, a limited series of five vehicles commissioned in 2009 by the Hong Kong importer, envisioned as the epitome of the Zonda lineage at that time.

Derived from the Zonda R, an uncompromising iteration engineered for track dominance, the Cinque boasted a formidable 678 bhp 7.3-litre engine paired with a brand new cutting-edge 6-speed robotised transmission. Its enhanced body, constructed from titanium-reinforced carbon fibre, ensured unparalleled rigidity, augmented by a suite of aerodynamic enhancements, plus a roof air intake. Configured thus, its on-road performance transcended the ordinary.

Crafted for the Hong Kong market, these Cinque originally featured a right-hand steering wheel configuration. Among them, the third iteration stands alone, resplendent in a vibrant and unique orange hue called Arancia St-Tropez, casting a dramatic contrast against the pristine snow-laden Swiss scenery that envelops it. Our journey traced a picturesque route from the summit of Col du Marchairuz in the Jura Mountains to the tranquil shores of Lake Geneva, a mere stone's throw from the cosmopolitan hub of Geneva.

Beyond its technical prowess and performance credentials, the Pagani Zonda has left an indelible mark on popular culture and the automotive world at large. Revered by enthusiasts and collectors alike, the Zonda has become a symbol of automotive excellence and aspiration, embodying the dreams and aspirations of those who dare to push the limits of possibility. ■

SOTTOZERO

PAGANI ZONDA CINQUE

2009
5 units produced (out of a total of 168 Zonda)
V12 engine (7,291 cc)
678 hp
350 km/h

ASTON MARTIN ONE-77

PERFECTING PERFECTION

DUBAI, UNITED ARAB EMIRATES

by Aston Martin

Like a mirage in the desert: there were only 77 examples of the One-77, which personified the very best of motoring for Aston Martin.

Born from the vision of Aston Martin's elite team of engineers and designers, the One-77, named for its limited production of just 77 units, represents a milestone in the marque's storied history. Conceptualised at a time when automotive enthusiasts hungered for something truly extraordinary, the One-77 emerged as a beacon of innovation and luxury. Its inception marked a departure from convention, as Aston Martin sought to redefine the boundaries of automotive excellence.

Set against the backdrop of the desert landscape of Dubai, the Aston Martin One-77 appears as a vision of automotive art. As the sun sets, casting a warm glow over the sands, the clean lines and distinctive silhouette of the One-77 create a mesmerising juxtaposition with the grandeur of nature. Every curve reflects the evolution of the sand, every detail a testament to timeless elegance, making this moment an eternal testament to the fusion of humanity and machine.

In a display of exquisite exclusivity, Aston Martin meticulously crafted a mere 77 specimens of the One-77, each distinguished by its bespoke specifications tailored to the discerning tastes of its patrons. Embarking on a mission of unrivalled sophistication, the renowned British manufacturer sought to birth not just a vehicle, but a legend – the inaugural supercar bearing the Aston Martin insignia, poised to captivate aficionados and redefine automotive excellence.

The One-77's construction ascended to the zenith of automotive artistry, solidifying Aston Martin's standing as a paragon of unparalleled craftsmanship and singular skill. Enveloped in a carbon-fibre monocoque chassis, its sculpted contours boasted hand-formed aluminium, showcasing unparalleled precision in its assembly. Notice, for instance, the rear section, devoid of any panel lines, and observe how the air intakes framing the car's muzzle seamlessly blend with the headlights, a testament to meticulous design integration.

In the realm of supercars, the One-77 boasts a rare architecture firmly rooted in Aston Martin tradition, being a front-engined GT. Beneath its elongated bonnet resides a formidable 7.3-litre V12 engine, an evolutionary marvel derived from the 5.9-litre powerplant found in the DBS, meticulously reworked by Cosworth with not a single component shared between them. It was paired with a cutting-edge 6-speed robotised transmission, while its suspension system adopts pushrods with horizontally mounted spring/damper units reminiscent of those found on racing cars.

Pushing the boundaries of Aston Martin's capabilities, the One-77 emerged as not only the most potent offering from the manufacturer, boasting a staggering 760 bhp, but also claimed the title of the fastest, clocking in at 354 km/h. With a price tag surpassing a million pounds, it stood as the epitome of luxury and exclusivity. Yet, for discerning clients, this

SEVEN
CAR LOUNGE

Carbon details abound, including under the bonnet, with the spectacular Y-shaped body reinforcement – when it came out in 2009, its 760 bhp V12 was the most powerful naturally aspirated engine in the world.

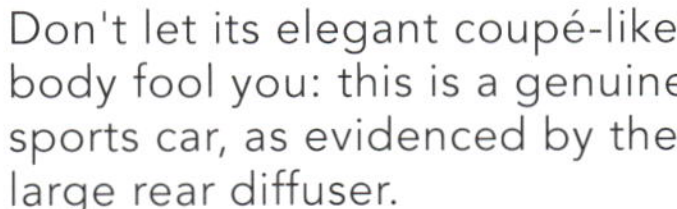
Don't let its elegant coupé-like body fool you: this is a genuine sports car, as evidenced by the large rear diffuser.

The red lip under the grille discreetly indicates that this is a very rare and exclusive Q-series One-77

pinnacle of automotive achievement was merely the beginning. At the conclusion of production, a select few, estimated to be seven in number, were entrusted to the esteemed 'Q by Aston Martin' programme – a nod to the mythical Q Division in James Bond movies – for further enhancements, ensuring that each car become a masterpiece of individuality and refinement.

Sold at a stratospheric price, exceeding double that of the standard models, each One-77 Q-Series iteration showcased specific exterior and interior hues, punctuated by striking contrasts. Take, for instance, this remarkable example adorned in Spirit Grey paint, elevated by a bold horizontal red stripe accentuating the front spoiler, complemented by a captivating two-tone red-and-black interior. Not stopping there, it boasts special black 10-spoke forged wheels, red-painted brake callipers and a myriad of carbon details, each element meticulously curated to elevate the aesthetic of this automotive masterpiece.

The majority of Q-series models now find their residence in Dubai. Among them, one standout has even taken on the prestigious role of a police car in this city of boundless possibilities. Amid the tranquil expanse of the desert, the Aston Martin One-77 awakens, its engine resonating with unbridled power, reverberating through the undulating dunes. Its formidable presence amid this untamed, unspoiled landscape is a sight to behold, a testament to the symbiotic relationship between supercars and the open desert expanse, where they truly find their natural habitat.

Even as time progresses, the One-77 perseveres as the paramount symbol of grand touring according to Aston Martin's ethos, representing a pinnacle achievement in the realm of traditional British motoring craftsmanship. Its enduring legacy serves as a testament to the meticulous artistry and engineering prowess that define Aston Martin's rich heritage. ■

ASTON MARTIN ONE-77 Q-SERIES

2009–2012
7 units produced (out of a total of 77 One-77)
V12 engine (7,312 cc)
760 hp
354 km/h

KOENIGSEGG AGERA R

EVIDENCE FOR THE EXISTENCE OF EXTRATERRESTRIAL LIFE

DUBAI, UNITED ARAB EMIRATES

288

N 288

Incredibly spectacular, and iconic of Koenigseggs: the dihedral synchro-helix doors pull away from the car as they pivot towards the sky.

The saga of the Koenigsegg Agera R unfolds as a testament to the audacious vision and relentless pursuit of automotive excellence by Christian von Koenigsegg and his dedicated team. Bursting onto the scene at the Geneva Motor Show in 2011, the Agera R swiftly etched its name into the annals of automotive history, embodying the apex of Koenigsegg's engineering ingenuity and unwavering commitment to performance.

Amid the vast expanse of the Dubai desert, the Agera R finds its canvas, its sleek silhouette cutting through the golden sands like a blade through silk. The harsh desert sun casts long shadows across the landscape, highlighting the Agera R's sculpted lines and dynamic presence. Here, in this realm of extremes, the Agera R thrives, its performance capabilities matched only by the boundless horizons that surround it.

Renowned for its avant-gardism, Koenigsegg is the paragon of innovation among supercar designers. When it unveiled its first marvel, the CC8S, in 2000, the Swedish manufacturer set the world alight with its radical technological solutions. Seemingly emerging from the ether, the CC8S was equipped with a bespoke in-house engine of formidable prowess, boasted an extraordinary top speed of 390 km/h, and was distinguished by its spectacular dihedral synchro-helix doors, which rose elegantly vertically. The CC8S was just the beginning of a fascinating odyssey that bears witness to Koenigsegg's unwavering commitment to redefining automotive excellence.

A decade later, having established itself among the automotive elite, sharing the limelight with the likes of Bugatti and Pagani, Koenigsegg unveils a new masterpiece that pushes the boundaries of what's possible even further: the Agera. Featuring a revolutionary 5.0-litre twin-turbo V8 engine, meticulously engineered in-house, the Agera unleashes a staggering 960 bhp, setting a new benchmark in automotive engineering. Coupled with a revolutionary 7-speed robotised transmission with paddle shifters, optimised by Koenigsegg's ingenious engineering, the Agera reached a top speed of 400 km/h, achieving a celestial level of performance. However, for the visionary minds at Koenigsegg, the pursuit of excellence knows no bounds. There was more to come.

The next step in Koenigsegg's relentless pursuit of automotive perfection came in the form of the Agera R, a marvel capable of a breathtaking 1140 bhp when fuelled by E85 bioethanol, transcending the limits of conventional fuel. Elevating aerodynamics to an art form, the Agera R has introduced an innovative active rear spoiler, whose pylons ingeniously double as chimneys to expel hot air from the engine compartment. Technical innovation remains the beating heart of Koenigsegg's boundless creativity.

Challenging the supremacy of the Bugatti Veyron, the Koenigsegg Agera R established itself as a formidable competitor, despite initial scepticism about

One of the original features of the Agera is the Ghost Lighting System of laser-engraved pictogram buttons that are invisible when the car is switched off.

Do nothing like the others: the uniquely shaped digital instrument cluster is configurable and can display a G-force meter or stopwatch.

the Swedish carmaker that produced only a handful of cars. However, a series of meticulously homologated world records served as a resounding response to the sceptics. The Agera R demonstrated its unrivalled prowess by accelerating from 0 to 300 km/h in just 14.53 seconds, earning its place in *Guinness World Records* for the remarkable 0–300–0 km/h performance in just 21.9 seconds. This impressive stopping power was achieved using meticulously engineered in-house brakes, demonstrating Koenigsegg's unwavering commitment to excellence in all facets of automotive engineering.

Each of the 16 examples of the Agera R carries its own specification, and this one emerges in a resplendent display: a captivating incarnation wrapped in the enchanting hue of Candy Apple Red. This is the inaugural Agera R, commissioned by the Royal Family of Oman – a masterpiece that would have been delivered before the model's public unveiling. As well as its unique colour, it features red-tinted carbon appendages, embodying a blend of elegance and individuality.

With its supersonic capability, soaring beyond 440 km/h, the desert serves as its perfect playground, albeit occasionally interrupted by graceful manoeuvres to evade the swirling sands stirred by the wind. As the spectacular doors unfurl skyward, their movement fluid and seamless, one might almost envision extraterrestrial beings emerging to tread this ethereal landscape, a testament to the otherworldly allure of the Koenigsegg Agera R.

As one might anticipate, Koenigsegg's journey did not culminate with the Agera R, as subsequent creations from the Swedish marque have eclipsed its power and performance figures. Indeed, the Swedes have ushered in a new era of automotive innovation, introducing patented technologies hitherto unseen in the realm of automobiles, and, indeed, anywhere else. The lingering question persists: is Koenigsegg not from a realm beyond our own, where ingenuity and creativity transcend earthly confines? ■

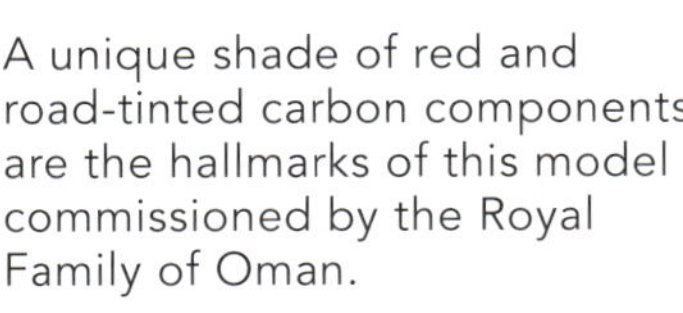

A unique shade of red and road-tinted carbon components are the hallmarks of this model commissioned by the Royal Family of Oman.

Have you seen the ghost (above)? This is the emblem of the fighter pilot squadron that used to be based at the former Ängelholm air base that is now Koenigsegg HQ.

KOENIGSEGG AGERA R

2011–2014
18 units produced (out of a total of 58 Agera)
V8 twin-turbo engine (5,032 cc)
1140 hp
442 km/h

PAGANI HUAYRA

EXCELLENCE AT THE AGE OF MATURITY

MONTE CARLO, MONACO

The Huayra in the pure elegance of its first iteration. But that doesn't mean it's simple: its bodywork, which functions like an inverted aircraft wing, features active flaps at all four corners

The saga of the Pagani Huayra began with whispers of anticipation that resonated throughout the automotive world. Named after the ancient Andean god of wind, this hypercar emerged as the successor to the illustrious Zonda. Its genesis was a long one, culminating in its grand debut at the 2011 Geneva Motor Show, where it captured the collective imagination of enthusiasts the world over.

In Monaco, where luxury and extravagance converge, the Pagani Huayra feels right at home. Against the backdrop of the iconic harbour, its sculpted lines and exotic presence draw the eye, reflecting the city's glamorous allure. Venturing beyond the city limits, the Huayra conquers the serpentine mountain roads with grace and precision, showcasing its dynamic capabilities among the breathtaking Mediterranean vistas.

In the midst of fervent competition and the relentless pursuit of automotive excellence, Horacio Pagani found himself pondering a delicate question: what could surpass the Zonda? Despite its exceptional qualities, the relentless march of progress threatened to overshadow his inaugural hypercar creation. The challenge was formidable, demanding eight years of painstaking effort to forge a new icon worthy of the Pagani legacy.

The new car echoes its illustrious predecessor in its exterior form, characterised by bi-xenon headlights and Pagani's distinctive exhaust system. However, its contours are now more fluid, embodying a more organic and sensual aesthetic. The captivating articulated gullwing doors add to its appeal – a show of genius. This feat has been achieved through the creation of an entirely new monocoque cell, surpassing the rigidity of its Zonda predecessor thanks to a titanium-reinforced carbon-fibre construction.

Under the bonnet, a significant shift occurred: AMG, the esteemed sports division of Mercedes-Benz, continued to furnish the V12s for the Huayra, albeit with a novel 6.0-litre engine bespoke to Pagani, meticulously crafted and hand-assembled in Germany. Diverging from typical AMG powertrains, this iteration boasted enhanced responsiveness in its turbos, dry sump lubrication, a titanium exhaust system and a host of other refinements, culminating in an output of 730 bhp and an even more spirited demeanour. Notably, it achieved the apex of efficiency in its sector, underscoring the Huayra's commitment to environmental conscientiousness amid its hypercar prowess.

Arguably, the most captivating aspect of the Huayra lies in its aerodynamic ingenuity: the entirety

778K

An unique interior: a mix of large machined aluminium parts, wide leather-trimmed surfaces and carbon-fibre elements create a retro-futurist vibe that could be described as steampunk.

In this avalanche of aluminium, note the ignition key, which reproduces the shape of the car in reduction. Impressive.

The 64th of the 100 Huayras is the first to use this type of beautifully aged leather: a special order that will be emulated by some.

of the car's bodywork operates akin to an inverted airplane wing. Its characteristics dynamically shift by altering the angle of incidence through adjustments in the front and rear suspensions, complemented by four active flaps strategically positioned at each corner. This sophisticated system not only modulates airflow throughout the car but also optimises weight distribution, ensuring peak performance across diverse driving scenarios. A similar meticulousness extends to enhancing the airflow for cooling various mechanical components and undercarriage circulation. True to its namesake, the Huayra emerges as a progeny of the wind, embodying a seamless fusion of aerodynamic prowess and automotive excellence.

Among the Pagani Huayras, numerous iterations have undergone modifications featuring more assertive body kits. However, chassis #64 remains a pristine exemplar, steadfast in preserving the car's purest essence. Painted in a refined Luci Del Bosco hue with gold rims, it exudes timeless elegance, accentuated by an interior clad in aged leather. Notably, it stands as the inaugural Pagani to incorporate such bespoke leather, a bespoke option subsequently integrated into the brand's repertoire. Its juxtaposition against the pale turquoise blue of Monaco harbour, a rare colour attributable to unique atmospheric conditions, renders a captivating harmony. In the epicentre of European opulence and supercars, our Huayra gleams resplendently, akin to a luminous pearl amid the prestigious enclave.

As the Huayra gracefully approaches the twilight of its illustrious career, it serves as a profound reflection on the evolution of hypercar engineering and design, as well as Pagani's enduring success at the zenith of the automotive hierarchy. With the emergence of the Ultima, a new car poised to succeed it, the Huayra remains an undisputed monument to grace and performance, etching its legacy in the annals of automotive greatness. ■

ATLANTIS II

Huayra

PAGANI HUAYRA COUPE

2011–2018
100 units produced (out of a total of 341 Huayra)
V12 twin-turbo engine (5,980 cc)
730 hp
360 km/h

LAMBORGHINI AVENTADOR J

DEFINING UNIQUENESS

PUERTO BANÚS, MARBELLA, SPAIN

The definition of exclusivity: this road-legal concept car, intended to be sold to one lucky owner only, foreshadowed the future Aventador Roadster, as well as the extreme SV version, years ahead of its time.

The Aventador J is a unique expression of automotive artistry, born from Lamborghini's rich legacy of innovation. Its open-top roadster design, unveiled at the 2012 Geneva Motor Show, marks a departure from convention, offering drivers an exhilarating experience of pure motoring freedom.

As the dawn breaks and the world awakens, the Aventador J remains a silent sentinel, a testament to the timeless allure of automotive craftsmanship and design. In this tranquil setting, where the gentle lapping of waves mingles with the distant hum of engines, the Aventador J transcends mere machinery, embodying the spirit of adventure and freedom that defines the Lamborghini experience.

This car arrived as an unexpected treat, a surprise in the midst of the grandeur of the 2012 Geneva Motor Show. It appeared not just as a concept, but as a visionary glimpse of the future roadster incarnation of the Aventador. Yet it was much more than a show car destined for ephemeral exhibitions and *concours d'élégance*, for Lamborghini, in a bold move, homologated it for the road. Built with meticulous attention to detail, it bore all the hallmarks of a production model, testifying to Lamborghini's unwavering commitment to excellence.

This singular creation was not destined for museum confines; instead, it found its place on the open road, sold to a discerning customer. With only one example ever assembled, it embodies the epitome of exclusivity – an unparalleled masterpiece revered for its rarity and distinction.

From a technical standpoint, this car mirrored the specifications of a production Aventador LP700-4 coupé, yet it was the form that truly astounded. Naturally, the absence of a roof catches the eye immediately, but equally striking is the removal of the windscreen, transforming the supercar into an authentic barchetta. The twin cockpit, delineated by a body separation, features a central rear-view mirror poised atop a mast, creating a distinctive divide.

Unique touches abound, with the spoiler and wheel rims bespoke to the car's design. In a nod to performance optimisations, amenities such as heating, GPS navigation, and audio systems were omitted in favour of weight reduction. This uncompromising approach underscores the Aventador J's dedication to pure driving exhilaration.

Transformed into a genuine racing car for the road, the Aventador J demanded only a helmet for those brave enough to take the wheel, and in cooler climates, even a wetsuit was advisable. The significance of the 'J'

The rear of this concept car has been redesigned, with unique details such as the carbon panel featuring the red-tinted Lamborghini brand logo.

The helmet supplied with the car placed on the rear wing. This one is specific, with upper surface twin mounts like on modern race cars.

in its name, pronounced as 'Yota', is indicative. It serves as a nod to Appendix J of the FIA regulations governing the homologation of competition cars, a testament to its racing pedigree. This designation also pays homage to the iconic Lamborghini Miura P400 Yota, named for similar reasons.

Since its unveiling in 2012, this extraordinary car, a prized jewel in one of the world's most exquisite collections, has remained elusive, gracing public view on only the rarest of occasions. Among these rare glimpses was its celebrated appearance at the Costa del Sol Concours d'Élégance in 2021, where it garnered accolades and admiration by winning the Best of Show award. The custodian of this masterpiece is Magna Supercars, a premier Spanish firm renowned for its expertise in the realm of automotive excellence, entrusted with the meticulous care of the Aventador J.

In the tranquil embrace of Puerto Banús, just a stone's throw away from the grandeur of the Concours d'Élégance, the Aventador J emerges in the early morning hours. This picturesque marina stands as the epitome of luxury in the Marbella region, the Monaco of the Andalusian coast – a treasure trove of opulence, adorned with the timeless charm of Spanish seaside heritage. Under the overcast sky, the roadster's distinctive crimson hue, accentuated by gleaming chrome highlights, creates a captivating contrast. With an aura akin to volcanic fury, this devilish car appears to emerge from the depths of hell, riding upon a molten flow of lava.

The legacy of the Aventador J remains unparalleled, even as Lamborghini's production line evolved to include more conventional Aventador roadsters, boasting windshields and two-piece electric roofs. By crafting this singular model and offering it to a fortunate patron, Lamborghini has bestowed upon the automotive world a masterpiece that will be revered for generations to come at prestigious motoring gatherings worldwide. An instant classic, the Aventador J stands as a timeless symbol of automotive artistry and innovation. ■

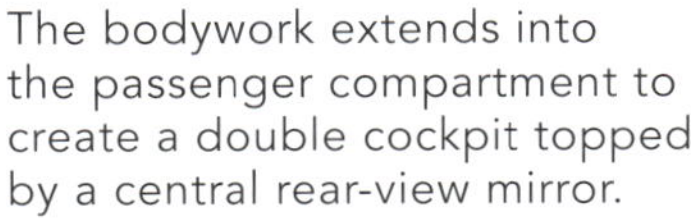
The bodywork extends into the passenger compartment to create a double cockpit topped by a central rear-view mirror.

J as in 'Jota', the magic Lamborghini letter for extreme models since the Miura of the same name.

LAMBORGHINI AVENTADOR J

2012
1 unit produced
V12 engine (6,498 cc)
700 hp
350 km/h

PORSCHE 918 SPYDER

THE SPEED OF LIGHT

MANAMA, BAHRAIN

62226

Reminiscent of its predecessor, the Carrera GT, the 918 Spyder has lines that appear to be carved from a block of molten metal set against rims that evoke electric motor rotors. An evocation of the high technology of this hybrid hypercar.

At the intersection of tradition and innovation lies the Porsche 918, a masterpiece born from the crucible of Porsche's racing heritage and technological prowess. With roots deeply entrenched in motorsport glory, the 918 inherits the legacy of legends like the iconic 917 and the timeless 911, each carving their place in the annals of automotive history. This lineage isn't just a lineage; it's also a promise – a promise of performance, precision and passion that defines the very essence of Porsche engineering.

In the nocturnal embrace of Bahrain's urban landscape, the Porsche 918 sets the night ablaze with its presence. Surrounded by the futuristic architecture that adorns the skyline, the lights of the city reflecting off its fluid bodywork, our car, with its sleek contours and aerodynamic profile, exudes an aura of determination and elegance.

Three decades have passed since the iconic 959 graced the automotive scene, and now Porsche emerges again with an ultra-technological hypercar, marking a new era in automotive excellence. This unparalleled masterpiece boasts a hybrid engine, redefining the concept of hypercars. Its revolutionary design enables seamless transitions to 100% electric mode within urban confines, while proudly showcasing top-tier fuel efficiency and CO_2 emission standards, setting a new benchmark in automotive innovation and sustainability.

Remaining faithful to the esteemed Porsche hypercar legacy, the 918 Spyder seamlessly merges a combustion engine with a storied racing heritage. Specifically, it inherits the illustrious V8 engine from the RS Spyder sports car, celebrated for its commanding presence in the LMP2 category from 2006 to 2010, ultimately securing victories at the prestigious 24 Hours of Le Mans in both 2008 and 2009. This mechanical marvel is harmoniously paired with an electric motor propelling the rear wheels, heightening power output, while an additional electric motor situated on the front axle enhances the car's capabilities, transforming it into a formidable four-wheel-drive wonder.

Within the intricate framework of this hybrid system lies a discreet yet powerful control mechanism nestled within the cabin. Through a single switch, you are granted the ability to select from an array of five driving modes, each tailored to your preferences: whether to embark on a serene journey powered entirely by electricity, embrace conscientious driving habits with minimal fuel consumption, or indulge in dynamic modes where electric motors unleash their formidable prowess to enhance racetrack performance. Yet, the technological marvels do not cease there; the vehicle proudly features active aerodynamics and rear-wheel steering, further enriching the driving experience.

With an unmistakable Porsche aesthetic, the 918 Spyder presents distinctly futuristic contours, boasting expansive, gracefully curved forms culminating in precise edges. As implied by its nomenclature,

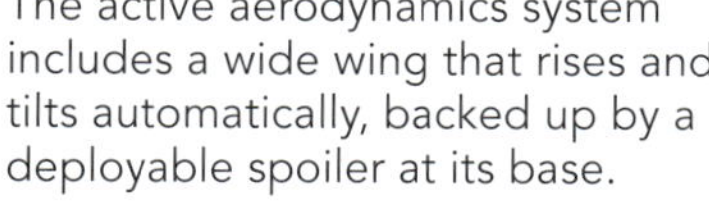

The active aerodynamics system includes a wide wing that rises and tilts automatically, backed up by a deployable spoiler at its base.

The car's most spectacular feature? The short tailpipes on top of the engine, just behind the arches of the rollover bar: watch out for the flames!

Ergonomics have been meticulously designed to master complex technologies: driving modes on the steering wheel, comfort and entertainment controls on the centre console.

The red interior is a rarity on the 918 Spyder: it lends a pleasantly nostalgic touch reminiscent of the Porsches of yesteryear to this ultra-futuristic hypercar.

it embodies the essence of a convertible, featuring a detachable roof. Notably, the pinnacle of its design lies in the vertical orientation of the tailpipes emerging from the rear bonnet, positioned just beyond the roll-over bars accommodating the vehicle's occupants.

In the balmy embrace of the Bahraini night, one effortlessly succumbs to the pleasure of hair-blowing drives, all while surrounded by the contemporary cityscape that mirrors the extraordinary technological marvels housed within the vehicle. The luminance of urban lights and neon accents cast ethereal reflections upon the sleek contours of the Porsche, evoking a sensation akin to a vessel sculpted from molten metal, reminiscent of scenes from futuristic epics. Embedded within the essence of the 918 Spyder lies an inherent affinity for radical modernity, an integral part of its genetic make-up.

To this day, the Porsche hypercar stands as a pinnacle of technological achievement in the realm of ultra-high-performance vehicles, remaining steadfast to the ethos instilled by the manufacturer since the inception of its inaugural masterpiece four decades ago, the 959. Among the illustrious 'holy trinity' of hybrid hypercars from the 2010s, the 918 Spyder etched its place in history, distinguished by its unparalleled utilisation of electric propulsion – a feat that balanced virtue and versatility while preserving the pure performance prowess inherent to the car. While the groundbreaking technologies it introduced have since become commonplace in contemporary hybrid sports cars, during its era, the 918 Spyder epitomised the zenith of its genre. ■

62226
البحرين
BAHRAIN

PORSCHE 918 SPYDER

2013–2015
918 units produced
V8 hybrid engine (4,593 cc)
887 hp
340 km/h

2013

MCLAREN P1

BORN IN THE PURPLE

TOKYO, JAPAN

品川000
ぬ 69-96

品川000
ぬ 69-96

Has a hypercar ever had such a complex rear end? Stunning when it was launched, the P1 has remained so: everything here is designed to optimise airflow, from engine cooling to aerodynamic downforce.

History intertwines with innovation as we delve into the legacy of the McLaren P1. Evolving from the realm of Formula 1 racing, McLaren Automotive embarked on a quest to redefine the boundaries of automotive performance with the P1. Introduced in 2013 as a limited-production plug-in hybrid sports car, the P1 captured the imagination of enthusiasts worldwide, setting new benchmarks for hypercar performance.

In the heart of Tokyo, amid the vibrant cityscape and under the delicate canopy of cherry blossoms, the McLaren P1 emerges as a testament to automotive excellence. This stunning fusion of cutting-edge technology and captivating design embodies the pinnacle of automotive engineering, seamlessly blending power, precision and aesthetics.

While McLaren's inaugural road car, the F1, stands as an incredible, iconic, and historically significant creation, it has often been viewed as a mere footnote for the British company primarily focused on Formula 1. Despite subsequently collaborating to produce the Mercedes SLR McLaren, it remained predominantly associated with Mercedes-Benz in the public eye, rather than serving as a successor to the F1. The concept of a large, front-engined GT did not align with McLaren's core ethos. It wasn't until 2011 that McLaren Automotive firmly established itself among car manufacturers with the introduction of the MP4-12C – a carbon monocoque, mid-engined sports car.

Fans still required patience before they could witness McLaren's re-emergence in the realm of hypercars. The spectacular P1, unveiled in 2013, caught the world off guard. Who could have anticipated that this nascent manufacturer would boldly venture into uncharted territory, pushing the boundaries of technological innovation with a hybrid engine hypercar? While the P1 did utilise the avant-garde carbon cell from the 'lesser' MP4-12C and its combustion engine as a foundation, the similarities ended there.

In keeping with its illustrious lineage, McLaren aspired for the P1 to embody the essence of a Formula 1 car tailored for the open road. This ambition began with the refinement of its twin-turbocharged 3.8-litre V8 engine, meticulously enhanced to unleash a staggering 727 bhp – the biggest specific output produced then by a production car. Inspired by Formula 1 principles, this combustion engine was perfectly integrated with a KERS electric system, linked to a compact battery. This synergy means that power can momentarily reach 903 bhp if required, without imposing significant additional weight.

Crafted entirely from carbon fibre, the meticulously sculpted bodywork of the McLaren P1 underwent rigorous wind-tunnel refinement, echoing the aerodynamic precision of a racing machine. A striking rear grille proudly exposes the engine, while a vast

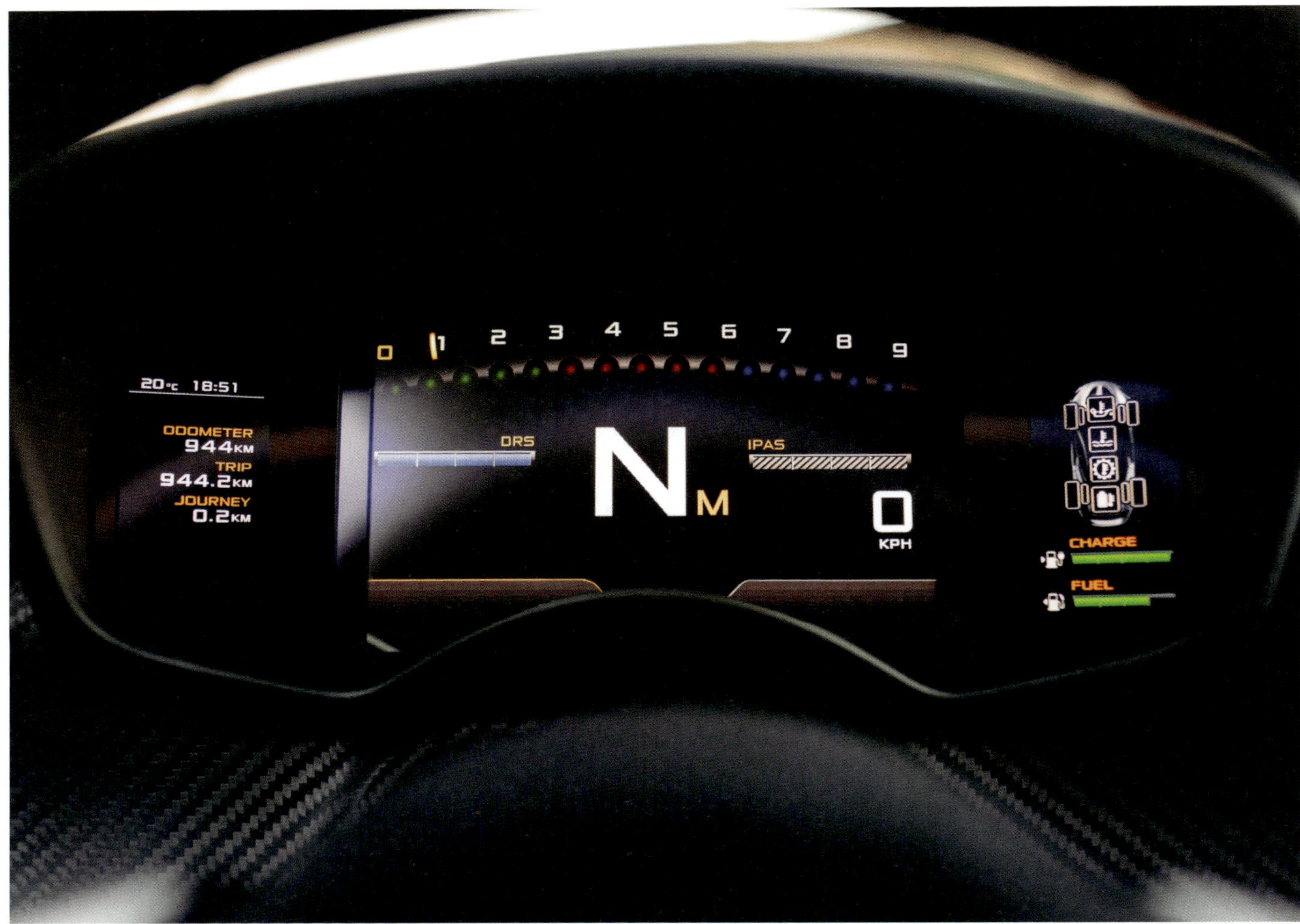

No frills: the instrumentation is straight to the point, just like on a race car.
It's better to avoid distractions at 350 km/h.

diffuser underscores the car's racing pedigree – a feat unprecedented in hypercar design, showcasing an open, sculpted rear end of unparalleled allure. Crowning this masterpiece is an imposing spoiler, meticulously engineered with a Formula 1–inspired DRS mechanism. Automatically adjusting at high speeds, it diminishes aerodynamic drag, propelling the car to even greater velocities. Inside, the P1 maintains its affinity with single-seaters, boasting a digital racing dashboard and expansive windows that afford astonishing visibility, further enhancing the driver's connection to the road.

Personalisation stands as a cornerstone of the hypercar ownership journey, and this particular P1 exemplifies bespoke luxury with its distinctive 'gourmet' aesthetic. Cloaked in a luscious Cadbury purple hue reminiscent of the iconic chocolate bar packaging, the theme extends seamlessly to the interior. Here, sumptuous chocolate-coloured leather, adorned with delicate white stitching (perhaps a subtle nod to a hint of milk) evokes the indulgent allure of confectionery.

In the bustle of Tokyo's streets, the vivid purple hue of the car creates a delightful contrast against the delicate pink of the cherry blossoms. With the sprinkling of petals gracefully adorning the pavement, the scene exuded an idyllic charm. Even seemingly trivial elements transport us to Japan, such as the ubiquitous drinks dispensers, their red accents adding another dimension of colour to the composition.

The McLaren name may have shone for half a century in motorsport, but the automotive industry remains a field where nothing is predetermined. McLaren was quick to establish itself as a road car manufacturer. However, with the P1, the company consolidated its return to the ultra-exclusive domain of hypercar production. The enduring legacy of the P1 lives on today, resonating with undeniable panache and reaffirming McLaren's esteemed position among the automotive elite. ■

Modern McLarens (above) have left their mark on the industry with their carbon-fibre structural bathtubs.

The unique Cadbury purple colour combined with a chocolate interior make this McLaren one to savour.

Coca-Cola
品川1000
ぬ 69-96
Coca-Cola
Coca-Cola

MCLAREN P1

2013–2015
375 units produced
V8 twin-turbo hybrid engine (3,799 cc)
916 hp
350 km/h

FERRARI LAFERRARI

ELECTRIC BLUE

LAKE GENEVA, SWITZERLAND

The name LaFerrari is the ultimate homage to the brand's glorious past, and the rear design evokes the glorious sports cars of the 1960s, but the hypercar's hybrid technology and active aerodynamics were downright futuristic.

The Ferrari LaFerrari, unveiled to the world in 2013, embodies more than just a leap in automotive technology; it encapsulates Ferrari's illustrious history and its relentless pursuit of perfection. The name 'LaFerrari' itself is a declaration, a statement that this isn't just any Ferrari; it is the embodiment of the brand's ethos, a culmination of decades of passion, expertise and innovation.

Nestled among the verdant vineyards of Switzerland, LaFerrari becomes part of the landscape, a work of art in the midst of nature's masterpiece. As the golden hues of autumn cover the landscape and the fresh breeze carries the scent of the grape harvest, the tranquil waters of Lake Geneva reflect the ethereal grace of the car, creating a visual symphony of contrasts and harmony.

With an iconic lineage stretching from the 288 GTO through to the F40, F50 and Enzo, Ferrari boasts an unparalleled succession of supercars and hypercars – a heritage steeped in automotive excellence. Yet, this rich legacy poses a profound challenge for the artisans of Maranello, who are tasked with surpassing past achievements, striving for heightened efficiency, and crafting vehicles that redefine automotive icons with each successive iteration.

The Enzo, a pinnacle of automotive engineering upon its debut, established a standard of performance and innovation that seemed insurmountable. However, in the ever-evolving landscape of high-performance automobiles, competition has intensified, with emerging marques poised to disrupt the dominance of established manufacturers. In the face of such formidable challenges, how could Ferrari continue to ascend to new heights of excellence?

With its evocative name, the LaFerrari boldly signalled Ferrari's commitment to deliver automotive excellence. The year 2013 witnessed a watershed moment in the realm of sports cars as hybridisation made a resounding entry, heralded by the emergence of the 'holy trinity' of hypercars: the Porsche 918 Spyder, the McLaren P1 and the Ferrari LaFerrari – the latter two unveiled simultaneously at the prestigious Geneva Motor Show. Yet each pursued a distinct path towards automotive innovation, the LaFerrari making the most moderate use of electric power, given that its naturally aspirated V12 engine remained an unrivalled benchmark.

This mechanical masterpiece was an evolution of the Enzo's engine, the last V12 designed by Ferrari, but whose power limits were pushed back to reach the staggering figure of 800 bhp, without the addition of any supercharging, true to the manufacturer's precepts. Instead, an electric KERS system, similar to that used in contemporary Formula 1 racing, could provide a further 163 bhp for a total of 963 bhp. Very light, the Ferrari's system was optimised simply for boosting performance: it was impossible here to drive in all-electric mode, but this development was planned for future models from the marque. The first hybrid to be assembled in Maranello, the LaFerrari acted as a test bed for the manufacturer's new technologies.

The rare Blu Elettrico colour combined with the equally rare 'Hermès' orange leather is one of the infinite possibilities offered by Ferrari's Tailor Made personalisation programme.

As in Formula 1: Ferrari pioneered the use of steering wheel controls, with its now famous Manettino. The LaFerrari plate is an area of personalisation at the owner's discretion...

Remaining faithful to the cherished tenets of Ferrari, the hypercar's bodywork was meticulously crafted with a singular focus on aerodynamic efficacy – a testament to the fusion of form and function. Every curve, every contour, was conceived with the precise intention of enhancing aerodynamic performance, whether to streamline airflow, diminish drag, or generate downforce essential for unparalleled stability and cornering prowess. Moreover, the intricate interplay of airflow dynamics was orchestrated not merely to cool or propel the engine but to optimise every facet of the car's performance. Within this meticulous engineering, however, lies a paradoxical challenge: to seamlessly integrate functionality with formal elegance – a hallmark of Ferrari's design philosophy.

In the realm of exclusivity, only a select trio of LaFerraris bask in the resplendent embrace of Blu Elettrico – extending even to their rear-view mirrors, typically swathed in bare carbon black. Yet, among them, one stands alone in its audacious addition of a Hermès leather interior in the brand's signature orange hue. A symphony of contrasts unfolds gracefully, mirrored in the choice of backdrop for its portrayal: the azure depths of Lake Geneva harmonise with the vibrant autumnal foliage of the Domaine des Combes vineyards. These hues, unexpected in the Ferrari lexicon, find their complement in the majestic Swiss peaks mirrored upon the lake's surface.

The LaFerrari stood as a beacon of technological prowess and significance. Today, Ferrari proudly boasts a comprehensive array of hybrid sports cars, each embodying the innovations pioneered by its hypercar predecessor, now made accessible to a broader audience. This transition marks a pivotal stride towards the imminent advent of an electric model – a crucial yet daunting endeavour for a manufacturer renowned for elevating the combustion engine to the status of a masterpiece, unlike any other. ■

FERRARI LAFERRARI

2013–2016
499 units produced
V12 hybrid engine (6,262 cc)
963 hp
350 km/h

2015

BUGATTI VEYRON LA FINALE

FAREWELL TO THE QUEEN

OJÉN, SPAIN

La Finale
PROVINCIA
DE MALAGA
OJEN

The circle is complete: the configuration of the latest Veyron, black and red, is the exact opposite of the very first Veyron produced, but with a bare carbon that was unimaginable when it was launched.

Introduced in 2005, the Bugatti Veyron revolutionised the automotive landscape, setting new benchmarks for speed, power and luxury. La Finale, unveiled in 2015, serves as the crowning jewel of the Veyron dynasty – a fitting tribute to a lineage defined by uncompromising performance and unrivalled craftsmanship.

Set against the rustic charm of the Spanish countryside, the Veyron La Finale exudes an aura of sophistication and dynamism. The winding roads of Ojén provide the perfect backdrop for showcasing the car's raw power and precision, as it navigates the picturesque terrain with effortless grace.

The Bugatti Veyron emerges as a testament to the visionary aspirations of the late Ferdinand Piëch, a titan of the Volkswagen Group during the dawn of the new millennium. Charged with the audacious mission of crafting the epitome of automotive excellence, Piëch sought to crown the group's illustrious portfolio, which now included revered marques such as Bentley and Lamborghini.

The Bugatti Veyron was conceived as a manifestation of automotive opulence and ingenuity that defied conventional limits, with three barely believable imposed objectives: a top speed eclipsing 405 km/h, surmounting even the fastest race car ever assembled; an awe-inspiring power output of 1,001 bhp, in a homage to the timeless tales of *One Thousand and One Nights*; and a demeanour that effortlessly whisked its occupants to the opera with unparalleled grace and refinement.

In essence, the Bugatti Veyron embodied the pursuit of automotive perfection – a harmonious synthesis of power, performance and poise that transcended mere machinery to become the ultimate expression of automotive artistry.

The project's genesis unfolded over a meticulous five-year span, from initial concept to the car's eventual debut. Crafting a vehicle where every detail flirted with extravagance proved an arduous task. At its core lay an engineering marvel: a 16-cylinder W-configured engine, turbocharged by four turbos. This feat involved the precise alignment of two WR8 engines, situated side by side on a shared crankshaft – an ingenious arrangement akin to V8s with exceptionally narrow angles.

Crafting a 7-speed dual-clutch robotised transmission to drive all four wheels and accommodate the staggering power and torque of 1,001 bhp and 1,250 Nm posed a monumental challenge. Equally daunting was managing the heat dissipation of a colossal mechanical system nestled within a relatively modest space, alongside the intricate development of brakes and tyres capable of withstanding such unparalleled performance. The Veyron ventured into uncharted territory, demanding meticulous attention to detail and innovation. Every component had to be meticulously engineered with unprecedented benchmarks in mind, pushing the boundaries of automotive technology to new heights.

Yet, this was merely the inception, as the car evolved into an even more surreal iteration, boasting an astounding 1,200 bhp, 1,500 Nm of torque, and a mind-boggling top speed of 431 km/h in its ultimate Super Sport guise. Naturally, such automotive mastery was entirely customisable, with boundless possibilities for

As it says in French, this is the *Veyron Finale*, the very last example of a car that has forever marked the history of the automobile.

A tribute to the past: the dancing elephant, sculpted by Rembrandt Bugatti, the brother of the manufacturer's founder Ettore, also featured on the legendary Royale of 1926.

customer requests – from breathtaking, intricate hand-painting to the incorporation of luxurious materials. The pinnacle of automotive engineering, the Bugatti Veyron stood as the epitome of opulence, exclusivity and desirability. It wasn't just the best car in the world; it was the most expensive and coveted, a true testament to automotive excellence.

The remarkable saga culminated with the Grand Sport Vitesse La Finale, marking the grand finale of the illustrious lineage of 450 Bugatti Veyrons. Paying homage to the iconic two-tone Veyron chassis #1, the Finale boasts a striking exterior adorned in two distinct carbon tones: black and red – a carbon hue unprecedented in Veyron history. The air intakes are elegantly tinted black, while the wheel centre caps, crafted from aluminium, proudly feature the signature sculpted Bugatti elephant emblem. Inside, the cabin is a masterpiece of luxury and sophistication, adorned in Hot Spur Red and Italian Red, with Silk Beige and red carbon accents adding an unparalleled level of refinement.

Since its unveiling at the 2015 Geneva Motor Show, the Grand Sport Vitesse La Finale has remained elusive and unseen – except once a year at the famous Costa del Sol Concours d'Élégance. Captured in Spain near the charming village of Ojén, renowned for its picturesque white-painted houses typical of Andalusia, this rare sighting comes to life with the assistance of specialist Magna Supercars. It's a privileged encounter with one of the most significant among the 450 Veyrons ever assembled.

The Veyron shattered the boundaries of the automobile, pushing limits to levels considered unattainable before Bugatti unleashed its magic. Although a handful of cars have since surpassed its legacy, this monumental milestone remains etched as one of the most pivotal moments in automotive history, a testament to Bugatti's unwavering quest for excellence and innovation. ■

A superlative instrument panel, with an unique power gauge topping out at 1200 hp and a speedometer graduated up to 430 km/h. Sitting here is an ultimate dream for many.

BUGATTI VEYRON 16.4
GRAND SPORT VITESSE

2012–2015
92 units produced (out of a total of 450 Veyron)
W16 quad turbo engine (7,993 cc)
1,200 hp
431 km/h

FERRARI MONZA SP1

NOSTALGIA ULTRA

MEGÈVE, FRANCE

What greater contrast could there be than a sports car with no windscreen or roof in the snow? But the 1950s racing cars from which it was inspired raced whatever the weather conditions. These are cars for heroes.

Born from the rich legacy of Ferrari's racing heritage, the Monza SP1 pays homage to the legendary barchette of the 1950s. Its name, Monza, evokes memories of the historic Italian racetrack where the Prancing Horse has triumphed time and again. Crafted as a limited-production marvel, the SP1 embodies the spirit of open-air motoring in its purest form, a true embodiment of Ferrari's commitment to automotive excellence.

Against the backdrop of the snow-covered Megève landscape, as snowflakes gently caress its sculpted curves, the Monza SP1 seems to have escaped from another era. The invigorating mountain air and the purity of the environment create a harmonious contrast with the SP1's flamboyant red exterior, underlining its imposing presence amid the tranquillity of nature.

Ferrari's Special Projects division has intricately woven a pivotal narrative in the marque's evolution from mere automaker to a paragon of luxury. It serves as an exclusive enclave, tailoring bespoke experiences for discerning clientele. Initially conceived to craft one-of-a-kind masterpieces for affluent patrons, the department has since ventured into crafting limited series commemorating significant milestones.

Enter the Monza SP1 and SP2, heralding a new chapter in exclusivity and craftsmanship. These models mark a departure, presenting the first production vehicles from the Special Projects domain. Despite their limited-series nature, they usher in an unprecedented volume, expanding the horizon of bespoke luxury within Ferrari's illustrious lineage.

The essence of Special Projects lies in the transformation of existing Ferraris into timeless masterpieces that echo the illustrious legacy of Scuderia Ferrari. What captivates the eye is the singular and enduring bodywork, reminiscent of the golden era of racing in the 1950s. Like its predecessors, it stands as a barchetta stripped of windscreen, windows or soft top, embodying pure driving exhilaration.

At its core, this creation embodies the ethos of racing purity – a vehicle designed for the sheer thrill of the open road. With its diminutive door granting access to a single-seater cabin, the SP1 epitomises exclusivity and intimacy in motion. Its counterpart, the SP2, extends a welcoming embrace with its passenger seat and expanded cabin, adorned with a second boss on the boot lid serving as a roll-over bar.

Yet, it is the SP1's unwavering dedication to its solitary driver that leaves an indelible mark. With only one seat, it offers a symphony of solitude, where every curve and contour are tailored to the individual behind the wheel. In its essence, the SP1 transcends practicality, embracing the purest form of automotive artistry.

Beneath the captivating silhouette of the SP1 Monza lies a harmonious fusion of heritage and contemporary Ferrari design ethos. Drawing inspiration from the iconic shapes of the 1950s, it seamlessly intertwines

megève
megève
MONZA SP1

The incredible Monza is available in two versions: the SP1, like this one, is a strict single-seater, while the SP2 allows you to be accompanied by a passenger. Either way, the atmosphere is minimalist.

The Scuderia Ferrari crest and its famous Prancing Horse – the emblem of a First World War flying ace passed on to Enzo Ferrari for his bravery at the wheel – emblazoned on the yellow of the city of Modena.

with the marque's present-day aesthetic, embodying a captivating synthesis of proportions and style. While its exterior pays homage to the golden era of racing, beneath the surface beats the heart of a thoroughbred: the chassis and powertrain borrowed from the acclaimed 812 Superfast. Positioned in the front, the 6.5-litre V12 engine unleashes a staggering 810 hp.

In its standard coupé form, the 812 Competizione already commands attention with its exceptional performance and dynamic prowess. However, the SP1 Monza transcends boundaries, offering an unparalleled driving experience that defies conventional limits. Imagine the rush of wind against your face, the unbridled sensation of symbiosis with the elements, as you navigate the open road with a panoramic view.

In the serene enclave of Megève, a chic ski resort nestled at the foot of the Mont Blanc massif, the unexpected allure of the SP1 finds its natural habitat among a clientele accustomed to the extraordinary. Here, amid the glistening snow-capped peaks and the hushed whispers of winter, in a place where luxury knows no bounds, the allure of indulging in a unique snow sport adventure becomes irresistible.

This particular SP1, the final creation of its kind, bears a sublime red paintwork that pays homage to Rosso Fuoco, Italy's traditional racing red. Gold wheels shimmer in the winter sunlight, while roundels eagerly await the imprint of racing numbers. Yet, it's the subtle details that truly captivate the discerning eye, such as the inscription gracing the radiator grille, a nostalgic tribute to the iconic Italian number plates of yesteryears. Elegantly etched, the word 'Prova' echoes the spirit of prototypes destined for the racetrack, not the road.

To be behind the wheel of the Monza SP1 is to embrace the essence of automotive freedom – a visceral connection between human, machine, and the boundless horizon. It's not just driving; it's a symphony of speed, style and unparalleled exhilaration. ■

VINTAGE

FERRARI MONZA SP1

2019–2022
499 units produced (SP1 + SP2)
V12 engine (6,496 cc)
810 hp
300 km/h

2020

MCLAREN SPEEDTAIL

RIDE LIKE THE WIND

MARBELLA, SPAIN

McLaren
MAGNA SUPER CARS

With its long, tapering tail and teardrop shape, the Speedtail pursues the quest for maximum speed with perfect aerodynamics, blending cutting-edge technology with the aesthetics of cars from the Golden Age. A car in a class of its own.

The McLaren Speedtail represents the pinnacle of the British automaker's dedication to engineering prowess and aerodynamic mastery. Inspired by the legendary McLaren F1, the Speedtail pays homage to its iconic predecessor while charting a bold new course in automotive design and performance. Crafted as a limited-production marvel, it embodies the spirit of uncompromising luxury and unparalleled speed.

Photographed among the lush greenery of the private garden of Magna Marbella, the McLaren Speedtail appears as a natural artefact with organic lines. The tranquil ambience serves as the perfect backdrop to showcase the Speedtail's futuristic design. Gracefully navigating winding paths and sun-drenched avenues, the Speedtail embodies the harmonious balance between man, machine and the natural world.

In the graceful lines of the McLaren Speedtail, we witness a symphony of form and function, in which aerodynamic principles dance with futuristic aesthetics. Each curve and contour are painstakingly sculpted to harmonise airflow, ensuring the Speedtail moves through the atmosphere with grace and efficiency.

Its elongated body, tapered rear and iconic teardrop silhouette are not mere design choices but deliberate expressions of aerodynamic excellence. The absence of conventional side mirrors speaks volumes about McLaren Automotive's commitment to efficiency, the mirrors replaced by integrated camera systems that seamlessly meld into the car's sleek bodywork, complemented by the striking fixed front wheel covers.

From its understated silhouette to its mesmerising dihedral doors and revolutionary rear wings, every detail of the Speedtail's design serves a singular purpose: to elevate performance while captivating the observer's imagination.

Beneath the surface, the McLaren Speedtail boasts an array of groundbreaking technologies designed to redefine the driving experience. At its core lies a hybrid powertrain, a twin-turbocharged V8 engine and an electric motor to propel it to staggering speeds. With a total power output exceeding 1,000 hp, the Speedtail accelerates from 0 to 300 km/h in 12.8 seconds, catapulting its occupants into a realm of pure exhilaration to a mesmerising top speed of 403 km/h.

Performance, however, is only part of the equation. The McLaren Speedtail also pushes the boundaries of automotive technology with its advanced aerodynamics and active dynamics systems. From its adaptive suspension to its cutting-edge active rear ailerons, the Speedtail constantly adapts to changing conditions, delivering optimal performance and stability at all speeds.

Inside the cockpit, the Speedtail offers a blend of luxury and technology, with bespoke materials and state-of-the-art infotainment systems designed to enhance the driving experience. From its minimalist dashboard to its panoramic glass roof, every aspect of the interior is crafted to envelop occupants in comfort and sophistication.

Above all, the McLaren Speedtail pays homage to its esteemed predecessor, the iconic McLaren F1, by embracing the distinctive central driving position

McLaren
SPEEDTAIL
MAGNA SUPER CARS

The engine's dual air intakes, separated by the third vertical brake light, are built into the roof so as not to disrupt the flow of air around the body.

As on its glorious ancestor, the McLaren F1, the driving position is central, which also makes it possible to slim down the cockpit and reduce its frontal area.

flanked by two side passengers – a hallmark of its lineage. Echoes of the F1 resonate in subtle details, such as the shape of the small door windows. McLaren Automotive even limited production of the Speedtail to a mere 106 units – the same esteemed number as all F1 versions ever assembled. This deliberate choice not only underscores the exclusivity of the Speedtail but also honours the heritage and legacy established by its predecessor, further cementing McLaren's position as a pioneer in the realm of hypercar engineering.

Bathed in the exclusive SLR Blue hue meticulously crafted by McLaren's MSO department, our model radiates an unparalleled vibrancy that captivates the senses. Inside, the interior unfolds in a refreshing palette, featuring a harmonious blend of light blue and pristine white leather.

It's as if the car extends an irresistible invitation to immerse oneself in the warmth of a Mediterranean evening along the picturesque Andalusian coast. Envision taking a leisurely dip in the azure pool waters before embarking on a serene stroll through the verdant gardens of this estate, a location chosen for us by Magna Supercars, the custodians entrusted with the care of this exceptional vehicle.

McLaren has embarked on an extraordinary journey with its hypercars, uniting them under the prestigious banner of the Ultimate Series. The iconic F1 and groundbreaking P1 have pushed the boundaries of automotive innovation and performance. The Senna, with its stripped-down design, is focused solely on delivering pure driving sensations. In contrast, the Speedtail emerged as a harmonious response, embracing elegance and sophistication in every curve and contour. Following suit, the Elva epitomised open-air exhilaration, and then came the Solus GT, a glimpse into the future of circuit racing. A question remains: what will be the manufacturer's next surprise? It's a mystery shrouded in anticipation: only time will unveil the next chapter in McLaren's story. ■

With the gearbox controls on the ceiling, the interior is airy. The instrumentation is rich in screens, not least for the retractable rear-view cameras that contribute to the aerodynamic purity.

MCLAREN SPEEDTAIL

2020
106 units produced
V8 twin-turbo hybrid engine (3,994 cc)
1,070 hp
403 km/h

2022

BUGATTI CHIRON PROFILÉE

THE LAST TITAN

PARIS, FRANCE

BUGATTI

The Chiron adventure comes to an end with a unique fixed-fin body for a model that puts driving pleasure at the heart of the experience.

The Bugatti Chiron Profilée marks a significant chapter in Bugatti's history: the culmination of an era defined by the legendary W16 engine. As the final masterpiece equipped with this iconic powertrain to grace the marque's line-up, the Profilée stands not only as the zenith of Bugatti's pursuit of unrivalled power and speed but also heralds the conclusion of a distinguished era for the manufacturer.

In the tranquil dawn hours, the deserted streets of Montmartre awaken to the commanding presence of the Bugatti Chiron Profilée. In this Parisian tableau, it symbolises more than just the end of a chapter; it embodies the enduring legacy of a marque whose influence transcends generations.

Transitioning from the iconic Bugatti Veyron presented a formidable challenge, yet with the Chiron the French manufacturer has accomplished the remarkable feat of transcending the boundaries previously set by its esteemed hypercar predecessor. At the heart of its evolution lies a new monocoque structure crafted from carbon-fibre-reinforced plastic. This sophisticated material renders the chassis not only lighter but also stronger. A defining feature of its bodywork is the circular separation of its profile, with the prominent rear grille serving as a conduit for dissipating the heat generated by its potent engine.

At the core of Bugatti Chiron's prowess lies the formidable four-turbocharged W16 engine. With meticulous refinement, Bugatti engineers have managed to extract an additional 300 hp from the already impressive powerplant, catapulting the Chiron's output to an astonishing 1,500 hp – reaching even 1,600 hp in select variants. Despite its monumental power, the Chiron's top speed sees only a modest increase to 420 km/h. However, this figure belies the true potential of the machine. Electronic limitations restrict its top speed, a measure imposed not by the car's capabilities but rather by the constraints of available tyre technology.

Within the Chiron line-up, Bugatti introduced the Pur Sport model, tailored for driving aficionados. Shedding 50 kg in weight, it boasts fixed aerodynamics and shorter gears to optimise acceleration and cornering, albeit reducing the top speed to 350 km/h. While exhilarating to drive, it may prove a touch too extreme for those who prefer a more refined experience. For them, Bugatti imagined the Profilée: offering the same advanced technical features as its Pur Sport counterpart, it delivered unparalleled comfort without compromising on performance.

Originally intended for limited production, the Profilée took an unexpected turn during its development. By the time it took shape, the planned 500 examples of the Chiron had all been sold, making it impossible to launch it as a production model. Sadly, the Profilée remained a singular creation, a testament to what might have been. This extraordinary car, the epitome of Chiron refinement, found its moment of glory in early 2023,

PLACE
DALIDA

The horseshoe grille is a Bugatti trademark, but in the early days of the brand it was more egg-shaped - for Carlo Bugatti, the father of founder Ettore, the oval was the perfect shape.

The sweeping curve that wraps around the car's sides, as if to split it in two – and so hide the engine's air intakes – is a sublime homage to the 1936 Bugatti Type 57 SC Atlantic.

when it was auctioned off to give everyone a chance to own it.

With its distinctive rear spoiler harmoniously extending the bodywork and the subtle modifications made to the front, the Profilée attracted attention at every turn. Its distinctive colours, Atlantic Silver and Royal Carbon Blue, were a particular highlight. Inside, the seats of the Chiron Profilée were covered in leather and fabric, a first and last experience for the Chiron.

Captured at the break of dawn, these evocative photographs serve as a poignant memento of the car's historic journey through Paris during the momentous auction. Officially commissioned by the manufacturer to commemorate this extraordinary event, the images encapsulate the essence of a fleeting moment in automotive history. As the city of Paris slumbers in the early hours, the summit of Butte Montmartre emerges as the perfect vantage point, offering a panoramic view of the sprawling French capital below. In this moment, there are echoes of the iconic 1976 movie *C'était un rendez-vous*, a cinematic masterpiece that immortalised a car's daring rampage through the streets of the city.

As the day progressed, the Chiron Profilée commanded the auction floor, ultimately fetching nearly €10 million – an unprecedented figure that crowned it as the most expensive new car ever sold at auction. This remarkable achievement confirms the unparalleled desirability of Bugatti's latest W16-powered masterpiece, as well as the enduring allure of hypercars in the hearts of enthusiasts worldwide.

For Bugatti, and indeed for the entire automotive industry, the narrative remains one of constant evolution and reinvention. As each chapter unfolds, new heights of innovation are reached, pushing the boundaries of performance and luxury to uncharted territories. With bated breath, we are all awaiting the unveiling of the next chapter. ■

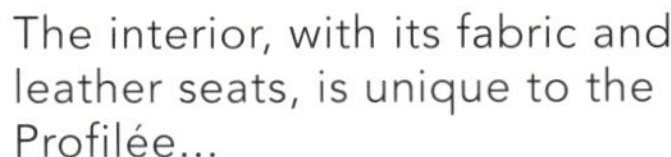

The interior, with its fabric and leather seats, is unique to the Profilée...

... as are its sculptural wheels, measuring 53 cm at the rear.

INTERNET

BUGATTI CHIRON PROFILÉE

2022
1 unit produced (out of a total of 500 Chiron)
W16 quad-turbo engine (7,993 cc)
1,500 hp
380 km/h

ACKNOWLEDGEMENTS

I cannot believe it has taken only just under a year from the initial spark of inspiration to the ultimate click of the camera shutter to the final book you have in your hands. Behind every image lies a strong network of support and inspiration, without which this project would not have been possible.

First and foremost, I extend my gratitude to Carolijn Domensino and her team from Lannoo for believing in me and including my vision. This project would not exist without you. Thank you.

To my friend Yan-Alexandre Damasiewicz for writing all these fantastic texts and making us feel the vibes of the photos through your words.

Thanks to Arthur Kar for the prefaces and believing in me since day 1.

Huge thanks to all the private collectors and organisations who entrusted me with their iconic cars. Thank you for allowing me the privilege of capturing their beauty and essence in stunning locations. Your generosity has enriched this book immeasurably: Davide & Andrea Parmegiani; Abdulla Faqeeh / Integrale; M.K.A.R / the_collection1; Arthur KAR / L'Art de l'Automobile; James Cottingham / DK Engineering; Enrique Ramallo / Magna Supercars; Selected Car Investment; Selected Car Collection; Drive Vintage; Seven Car Lounge; Shinji Takei / BINGO Sports International; Caretakers Collection; Don Huayra; Artcurial; Bugatti; RM Sotheby's.

Behind the scenes, there is a team of unsung heroes whose contributions have been indispensable. Your efforts have played a vital role in bringing this vision to life: Laurent André, Nikolaj Jeppesen, Jassim Keshi, Aaron Chung, Anna Fennel, Jeremy Rollet, Jonathan Meignan, Arnaud Singernberger, Chris.

Special thanks to my wonderful fiancée Sophie, my best friend, Arthur, and my parents, Eric and Fabienne. Thank you for your unwavering belief in me and support. Your love and encouragement sustain me to seek out new perspectives and push the boundaries of my craft.

Lastly, I extend my heartfelt appreciation to the readers who embark on this visual journey with me. May these images ignite your imagination, evoke emotions, and stir your passion for automobiles still further.

Kevin Van Campenhout

Text Yan-Alexandre Damasiewicz
Editing Léa Teuscher
Photography Kevin Van Campenhout
Book design Han van de Ven

Sign up for our newsletter with news about new and forthcoming publications on art, interior design, food & travel, photography and fashion as well as exclusive offers and events. If you have any questions or comments about the material in this book, please do not hesitate to contact our editorial team: art@lannoo.com

D/2024/45/327 – NUR 462/656
ISBN 9789401411295
3d print run

www.lannoo.com